S. FAXON AND THERESA HALVORSEN

Lost Aboard

Tales of the Spirits on Star of India

NBBP

This book is dedicated to the unseen crew of Star of India, both past and present. And a special cheer to the incredible crew maintaining her to this day.

Contents

Foreword

In November of 1863, when *Euterpe* (*Star of India*) was launched, there were about 10,000 large ships in British registry. *Star of India* is the sole survivor.

That *any* of them would survive should be surprising, for the maritime actuarial tables of the day used by marine insurance underwriters predicted a lifespan for a ship of her size and construction of about 12 years. Indeed, that was about the experience for each of *Euterpe's* three iron sisters also built by the Ramsey shipyard in Isle of Man. It wasn't necessarily that they always wore out in use or became obsolete, but that ships like *Star of India* operated in dangerous circumstances that argued against the expectation of a long working life. The spectrum of dangers were considerable: fire, collision, grounding, storms and hurricanes, navigational error, severe and crippling damage, mutiny, entrapment in ice, and finally if a ship survived all of that, the accumulation of wear, neglect, obsolescence and irrelevance to their surroundings. Any one of these things would have been sufficient to kill each of the 10,000 large sailing ships that shared her moment of entering the world, and indeed *did* kill all but one. *All* of those things happened to *Star of India*, and despite that and in defiance of the expected she is with us still, and is sailing still, a living thing.

Star of India is thereby, one of the last, if not the last, authentic physical emissaries from another world that has now faded far beyond all living memory. Our historians, docents, and educational staff have taken on the task of loaning her their voice in efforts to reconstruct that vanished world and channel her stories. Usually, these narratives derive from traditional sources familiar to historians: records, news articles, logs, diaries, letters, commercial documents, oral histories, plans and drawings, photographs, documentary art, and of course the ship herself as a physical repository of information about how things were once done.

But there is another category of story from *Star of India* deeply embedded in the culture of her world of long ago, and projected forward, of the culture of the ship herself as it continues evolving in lives shared by those of us who try to explain her. I am speaking here of the world of paranormal phenomena, a category of perceptual experience that during her early life was ardently embraced and believed in by vast swaths of western society, from common people to world leaders. While no knowledgeable person in 1863 would have dared think it likely for a ship like *Star of India* to last for a century and a half and still be sailing, most educated people of her day would have thought it a normal thing that any ship might be inhabited by ghosts, and that stories of encounters with such spirits would accumulate over time. These stories would simply linger into experience and memory, told and retold alongside the stories of harrowing storms, difficult passages, and eccentric characters until there was no one left who remembered long-gone ships or thought strange stories about them mattered anymore.

Except that as *Star of India* herself lived on, so did those stories in their entire exotic range, and they continue to be the stuff of not only memory but of experience, just as they always were. All of our crew understand, remember, signify, and interpret the experience of sailing the ship and listening to the curl of water from her bow and the moan of the wind in her rig as she heels to its power, as though sensing those things channeled through another life. To express this notion does not surprise anyone or conjure disbelief. But some of us who continue to serve her also experience and remember more ephemeral aspects of her distant world and, perhaps shockingly, some of the souls who once inhabited it. Those stories are not so comfortably shared because that portion of *Star of India's* world is no longer properly considered a rational part of ours. In our own world, these are strange sources. Yet they are her stories too.

So, do find a nice spot with a comfortable and cozy seat by the fire. For there's a few tales we want to tell you.

-Raymond Ashley, Ph.D., K.C. I., President /CEO of the Maritime Museum of San Diego

Acknowledgement

Ships like *Star of India* are alive in many more ways than imaginable. The sailors, fishermen, travelers, and even the tourists have grown and fortified their beings, their stories, and their emotions, creating an unseen aura aboard. Stepping onto *Star of India*, the past heavy on your shoulders, you can nearly see their shadows, hear their voices, feel what they felt. Many of these individual souls remain aboard, affecting the living, though their physical forms passed long ago.

There is no question *Star of India* is one of the more haunted ships still afloat, with active entities on every deck. Multiple blogs, articles, and even ghost-hunter shows have well-documented encounters. We gathered the experiences in this book from various staff aboard *Star of India.* Many of their own stories with the ship are over forty years old.

But we have to ask, why is *Star of India* so paranormally active? What makes *Star of India* different from other ships? Did the engineers and shipbuilders give *Star of India* a soul? Did she grow and change based on the storms, the collisions, and captains commanding her as a child would with changing guardians? Or was it the sailors, travelers, emigrants, stowaways, and fishermen who changed her, grew her into a separate entity? Was it their hopes, their dreams, their stories that shaped *Star of India's* soul?

So what is *Star of India's* soul like? After everything that's happened to her, has she become a beacon, providing a home for lost souls, both dead and living?

Having met many of the volunteers, we would say that her spirit is caring, motherly. Though she no longer carries passengers to new lands, today she brings the hopes and dreams of countless visitors and volunteers, looking for a window into the past. Volunteers, who themselves may feel a little lost, have found refuge in *Star of India*. Like so many souls before.

We have taken some liberties in bringing these stories to life, though we've done all we can to be accurate. Most of *Star of India's* ghost stories are oral traditions, written down after the fact and, we admit, likely embellished. Our goal is to bring the lost souls' stories, both how they lived and how they continue to haunt, into the light of day. We hope these stories may provide insight as to why *Star of India's* soul calls and provides refuge to lost souls.

Star of India circumnavigated the world 21 times using sail power alone and today enjoys her retirement as the flagship of the Maritime Museum of San Diego. The sisters in her fleet include the 1898 ferryboat, *Berkeley*, the 1904 luxury steam-yacht, *Medea*, the 1914 San Diego *Pilot* Boat, the 1984 topsail schooner, *Californian*, who is the official flagship of the Golden State, the 1970 replica of the 18th century Royal Navy frigate *Rose, Surprise*, the Vietnam Era Swift Boat, the replica Spanish Galleon *San Salvador,* the USS *Dolphin*, and the Soviet-Era Submarine, *B-39*.

Thank you to those who shared their stories with us and helped us bring this book to life. This story would not have been possible without Dr. Raymond Ashley, Kori Crossno, Jim Davis, Jenny Grepe, and John Merrill. We greatly appreciate your time and energy and acknowledging that those frightening moments made great stories. With the exception of one story and of our author Sarah, who has personally experienced the paranormal aboard *Star of India,* in their stories and of those who have been passed on through the years, we have changed the names of those who have shared their experiences. Any errors made are ours and ours alone.

As we say on crew, after an excellent day of sailing, here's to cheating death!

-Sarah and Theresa

Map of Star of India

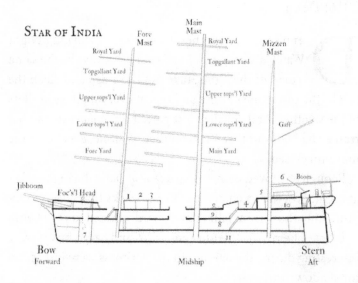

1) Cook's Cabin, 2) Galley, 3) Sailmaker's Cabin, 4) Main Deck, 5) Poop Deck, 6) Companionway, 7) Chain Locker, 8) Orlop, 9) Tween Deck, 10) Saloon, 11) Bilge.

Three Ghosts - One Night

2016: Demi

Demi's trainer told her every shift of working Night Watch aboard *Star of India* would always be the same. Turn off the lights, take out the trash and clean the heads (the restrooms). Rinse and repeat every night regardless of the weather. And, for the most part, it was that easy. But her trainer had left out that she wouldn't be alone, even after the museum closed.

Though she loved being aboard *Star of India* during the day, at night, everything changed. The bulwarks that felt friendly, protecting those from falling overboard, seemed to cage her in at night. The rooms full of ropes, sails, and cargo boxes were interesting during the day, but in the darkness were just places for shadowy things to hide.

Star of India was in the process of having her main deck replaced. The crew had built temporary structures to allow safe boarding on and off the ship. The bridge stretching across the width of her main deck by the saloon creaked and moaned with every step she made as Demi brought the trash bags from the lower decks to store besides the large bags topside.

Collecting trash and cleaning was relatively easy, but the recurring feeling of something watching her made her want to get the job done as fast as possible.

Tonight felt heavier than normal, those eyes noting her every move, every twitch. Demi found herself sweating despite the cool breeze off the San Diego Bay as she finished the final wipe downs. Next was the duty she dreaded; going down to the orlop deck (see map) to switch off the lights below.

When her feet descended the ladder to the long-planked orlop, she flicked the lights off. Like she had every time before, she looked forward, toward the bow, to ensure the lights were off. Darkness greeted her with a faint memory of the emigrants from the late 1800s who would have spent three months aboard, living on this deck with nearly no sunlight and only tiny portholes to catch glimpses of the surrounding seas. A creeping chill fell upon her shoulders, freezing the sweat dribbling down her back. She flicked off the light middeck then hurried up the two ladders to the main deck, keeping her eyes on the steps, out of the darkness in front of her. Other staff had told her they'd seen shifting shadows in the darkness, heard sounds they couldn't explain. She didn't want to risk experiencing any of those tonight. Not when the past felt so present.

Or any night, for that matter.

After running up the two ladders, panting, Demi shut the two wooden doors, sealing the deck below. She let out a slow exhale, but the tension in her shoulders did not lessen.

She had to check. It was almost an obsession.

Her feet crept toward the cargo hold, the square hole in the vessel's heart looking down through two decks. Her fingers landed atop the cold metal railing that kept people from stepping into the hole. The chilled touch of the metal upon her skin wasn't what sent bumps to rise upon her flesh as she looked down. The lights she'd turned off were back on.

Demi shook her head and said into the night, "Three nights in a row?" And just like on those previous nights, she thought, *Nope. I'm not going back down there. The next shift can turn them off again. If whatever is down there wants them on, then they can stay on.*

She tried to loosen her shoulders, aching with tension. The back of her shirt was soaked through with cold sweat.

She headed toward the bow, pulling a black trash bag out from her belt. The crackle of the plastic was loud in the cool night. She wiped the sweat from her brow as she passed the Cook's Cabin (see map), a window she did not dare look into at night. There was something off about that room, but she couldn't quite place her finger on what.

The trash can forward on the main deck wasn't as full as the others had been, so she decided to leave it in its can until she was ready to leave the ship. "Not dealing with that yet," she said aloud to the wind and anything else listening. She walked back toward the middeck where the main trash can and other bags were. Though she kept her eyes straight, Demi saw the soft glow of light emanating from below.

She dropped off the garbage load beside the open, full can, the rank of the day's garbage hitting her nose. Deciding to wait to tie it off until she was ready to leave, Demi proceeded under the temporary bridge into the saloon. Her steps passed the First Mate's Cabin, another opening she refused to look in. A man had committed suicide in there a century ago, and everyone said his spirit remained trapped inside that cabin.

She gulped, then returned to work, moving on to the saloon to

4

start wiping the long wooden table where the officers and first-class passengers had eaten their meals when *Star* was active. With her hands sweeping the rag across the luminous face of the table, two tugs pulled her hoodie. Demi shook her head.

Nope. Nothing there. Nothing trying to get my attention. She'd caught her hoodie on a non-existent nail or a sliver of wood. That was totally it.

The sound of footsteps creaking on the temporary bridge made Demi jump. She yelped.

Jesus, it's probably just Dan. The other security team member liked to use the head in the saloon on his break, and this wasn't the first time he'd startled her. She looked at her watch. 10:07 shone at her.

Dan doesn't take his break until 10:30.

She swallowed down the lump in her throat.

Probably just some homeless guy. Though the last thing she wanted was to chase a stowaway off the ship.

Summoning her courage, Demi hollered, "Hey. The ship's closed!" She began to walk toward the temporary bridge, hoping her voice would be enough to scare someone.

The footsteps stopped.

That's right, get off my ship.

Silence pursued.

Or just stay there, like a creeper.

She slowly stepped out from under the bridge and looked up, her heart racing.

No one. No shadows, no dark silhouettes in the night. Just the San Diego moon and stars.

No way. There's no way someone could have gotten away. It's gotta be Dan being a dick. Maybe he jumped to the poop deck? Without making any sound...that could totally happen, right?

5

Even her mental voice shook with the strain.

No one was going to play a joke on her. Raising her chin and squaring her shoulders, Demi rushed up the ladder to the bridge, each step echoing loudly across the empty ship.

"Dan, stop messing with me. It's not funny," she yelled ahead.

Her feet landed on the varnished and scarred wood of the poop deck. No one.

Maybe he's hiding behind the companionway?

With slow, measured steps, Demi proceeded aft, toward the companionway. A man could easily be hiding there, but why? Her hands shook, and she stuffed them into the pockets on her hoodie before forcing herself to keep walking.

Just before she reached the end of the structure, light shining from the gangway leading to the museum's ferryboat *Berkeley* caught her eye. Dan stood on the well-lit gangway, more than a hundred feet away, closing up the other boats.

Holding her breath, Demi looked around the companionway. Still no one there.

Alright, I'm done.

She rushed across the poop deck, across the temporary bridge, and down the ladder to grab the last bag out from the can and start hauling the garbage bags off the ship.

Reaching the main deck, she gasped and rocked to a stop.

The overloaded trash can was empty. Someone had added a new bag to the pile she'd left behind. Someone or something had finished collecting the trash for her.

Demi whipped around, searching for the helpful prankster. No one.

Gulping, she whispered, "Thanks?"

Though they were cumbersome, Demi grabbed all four bags and hauled them off the ship, ending her last night as Night

Watch aboard *Star of India*. The next morning, she requested a different position at the museum, one that didn't require being alone aboard the ship at night.

Author's Note:

It took us some time to deconstruct Demi's story as the entire evening was a frightening affair for her and very complex. As we've gotten to know the entities aboard Star of India, *and their stories, we've concluded Demi encountered three separate entities in one night, a record no one else we spoke to could beat.*

- *The footsteps on the temporary deck and in other places are a trademark of Captain Storry (Chapter 3)*
- *The tugging on her hoodie and the trash being tied up was likely Johnny both teasing and helping her (Chapter 2)*
- *The lights being turned back on was likely done by the spirit historically named "Chinyman" (Chapter 5), a denigrating term we address in his chapter*

Demi had several more encounters with spirits aboard Star of India, *including one with Captain McBarnett (Chapter 1) and even one aboard the Ferryboat* Berkeley *(see our website for that story).*

We want to give Demi an extra shout-out for sharing these stories that were so frightening to her. We can't tell you how much we appreciated it and had some sleepless nights ourselves, processing this story.

Lost at Sea: McBarnett

1979: Bobbie

Bobbie did his final walkthrough on the *Star of India*. The tallship had been his home for the last year. He didn't know what he would've done without the kindness of his boss for letting him live aboard. Now he had the most fantastic home he'd ever had, an entire ship from the 1860s to run around.

Sure, rowdy drunks visited the surrounding streets of downtown, and he heard rats running around the deck every other night. But *Star* was his, the rocking of the boat lulling him to sleep every night and the diamonds of dawn upon the water greeting him every morning.

Almost time for bed, he told himself after doing a final walkthrough of the decks.

The fog was rolling in, and the ship rocked harder than it had all day.

Storm must be coming.

He locked all the doors and went down to the saloon, the long room first-class passengers' from the late 1800s had eaten and socialized in. The long wood table, an antique by now, dominated the room, the tiny cabins people had slept in, surrounding it. A stained glass window of Euterpe herself let in the silvery glint of moonlight, and in its light, he could almost see the first-class passengers and crew who had sat at the table, laughing, drinking, and eating.

Bobbie flicked on the lights and the image faded. Grabbing a seat at the table, he pulled a notebook from his backpack, lifted a pencil, and flipped the pages to his algebra homework. Being in high school with a job as fantastic as this seemed so ludicrous, but his mother would kill him if he didn't graduate.

Bobbie did a few math problems, falling into a routine.

A soft sound in the room made him look up. He froze.

Leaning on a bulkhead to the left of him was a dark shape wearing a top hat.

His brain stumbled.

A top hat? Who wears a top hat nowadays? And how did he get inside? I locked the door!

He hadn't caught anyone aboard in weeks, and he'd been doing his patrolling. Besides, the homeless didn't wear top hats.

Before he could challenge the intruder, the shape turned, went down the hallway, through the closed door he'd just locked. How had someone gone through a locked door without opening it? The...person? Thing? Whatever it was had literally walked through a closed door.

Before he could do anything, the shape reappeared, went into the first mate's cabin, and disappeared again.

Bobbie flew into his cabin, closed, and locked the door, wondering what good that would do against a ghost.

So much for getting his math homework done.

1875: McBarnett

Captain McBarnett did not want to go. New Zealand sounded so primitive, so beneath him that the very idea of being restationed there as an "honorable" alternative made his skin crawl. He had fought his father, his superiors, in every way he could, but no. They said this was the only way to save his family and His Majesty's Army the humiliation for what he'd done.

But what did they know? They hadn't proven anything. Not really. But a mere few whispers against his conduct was enough to change his future. A few people who couldn't keep a secret and embellished the truth. And for what? To spare his family the humiliation of who he was?

It sickened him.

The men sent by his father had dragged him from the nearest tavern and, grabbing him by the elbows, marched him aboard. He'd managed to grab the bottle of Scotch he'd paid for on the way out though, so that was something, at least.

Once his feet hit the deck, the men had dropped his elbows, though he remained barely able to stand or balance his rucksack over his shoulder. The stench from the River Thames surrounded him, surrounded the ship, and made him want to gag. He muttered a thousand curses to his father, to propriety, to the idea his family could exile him like this. He looked up toward the sails, the white billowing bits of cloth that would take him to his fate.

Once in his room, McBarnett closed his eyes, hoping the cramped bunk would disappear when he reopened them. But the rocking of the boat made his head swim and his stomach heave. He cracked his lids open.

The room, barely big enough for a bed and a stool, hadn't

changed. Under the tiny window, a dark water stain did not portend well at its effectiveness in keeping rain or seawater out. He threw his rucksack to the foot of the bed and stood in the center of the room. With his arms outstretched, he cleared the bulkheads with no more than an inch from his fingers. He looked upward. If he put his top hat on, it would smoosh against the roof. How would he dress for dinner?

"You'll be in first-class the entire way," his father had told him.

"Bollocks," he'd said then and now. He'd seen single latrines larger than this. Raising his silver flask to his lips, he emptied it. He sucked in air through his teeth, though less from the sting of the whiskey and more from the disappointment it was gone.

Throwing himself into the bed, his back smacked into the wood supporting the bunk's thin mattress. He crossed his arms tightly over his chest, his eyes searching the lines of white-painted planks above him.

"I will not go to New Zealand." McBarnett's whisper was as ironclad as the hull of the ship.

The First Mate's cabin.

2017: Demi

Aside from hauling all of the booze, beer bottles, and ice to *Star of India*, the evening's event was looking straightforward. The event coordinator had Demi stationed out of the First Mate's Cabin, tending bar. Demi had pushed the single chair aside to make room for all the liquor and accompanying paraphernalia. She wondered if those who had slept here had ever thought their berth would become a bar. But this was an ideal place for it. Having four walls surround her and the alcohol sounded great. Hands of those drinking had a way of sneaking behind the bar in search of sips to steal.

Demi spent the hour before the party setting up the bar to her liking, and it wasn't long before the first of the guests arrived. She handed out plastic glasses of San Diego craft beer and measured out the cocktails with ease. However, after pouring the third whiskey sour, a strange sensation made her stop. Something wasn't right.

Something watched her.

Demi glanced over her shoulder. Only a tight, empty room peered back.

But how could anyone get behind her? The bar filled the entire doorway and there was no way anyone could be hiding behind her.

Relax. There's no one in here with you. Nothing weird has happened to me since I used to work Night Watch and there's a ton of people on board. It's going to be ok.

More guests appeared, and she went back to pouring drinks, glasses of Temecula wine this time, but the feeling of eyes upon her intensified.

Finally, she turned around.

There was nothing but a bunk, the cases of liquor, a chair, and a simple desk in the room with her. Of course, there was no one. It wasn't possible anyone could've ended up behind her. With a shrug, she helped the next customer, pouring four rum and cokes.

The customer walked away, and a lull came to the bar. She'd finished the orders for the first rounds, and the guests would need some time before coming back for seconds. The hum of the party became intermixed with the techno music thumping on the deck above her. Demi pulled out her cell phone to check the time.

Reflected in the glass of her phone, peering over her shoulder, were a pair of eyes.

Demi whipped around.

No one.

Heart pounding, she looked at the porthole on the opposite side of the cabin. There was no way anyone could be there. The ramp to board the ship was way above the line of sight. But someone was watching her. She saw it!

Trying to shake off the feeling, she searched the tiny room, even opening the large cabinet just in case someone was hiding within.

A guest tapped the bar, interrupting her search. Demi jumped.

"Can I get a gin and tonic, please?" he asked.

Demi nodded and obliged, happy for the distraction from the pressure of the eyes on her neck.

With over two hundred people aboard, the ship was alive with music and laughter, but Demi felt only one presence bearing upon her. It stared and whispered to her, though she couldn't make out the words.

It wanted something, something she couldn't give. Sweat broke out beneath her arms and trickled down her temples. More partygoers appeared, and she focused on making drinks, distracting herself by playing on her phone between orders.

But the feeling never went away.

Someone hungrily watched her hands pour drinks, staring as she bent over to place tips in the jar. Observing her as she poured various liquors and mixers into the plastic glasses and handed them over.

She soon gave up smiling at the attendees. She wanted to get out of here.

The tips may have been great that night, but she never wanted to be in that room again.

1875: McBarnett

It was the screams that woke him. The high-pitched squeals of the lower class passengers below his deck. He'd seen some of these people, the ones that couldn't afford the "first-class" cabin he slept in. No better than sidewalk sleepers they were, with their thick woolen skirts and dirty hands. When *Euterpe* had cast off in London, one of those children had sung a hymn to wish them well. Or he thought the sounds the child had made were supposed to be singing.

This trip was worse than he could've imagined.

First, the constant swaying, rolling, and rocking of the ship, no matter how micro or massive, left him longing for the predictability of land. At least when his head was spinning from drinking, the rest of the process was enjoyable. Second, the foghorn sounded for multiple days, keeping him from sleeping, and now, the screaming and moaning of the other passengers. He cursed his father again. First-class trip? Adventure in New Zealand? Pushing his legs out of the berth, he let them dangle, running his hand over his bearded face. He needed a shave, but why did it matter? There was no one here who cared what he looked like, who he was, who his family was. When he got to New Zealand, what was he going to do? Raise goats and plant potatoes? Sully himself marrying some uneducated vagrant?

He took a sip from the bottle he'd stolen from another passenger. It was almost gone. Then what? It wasn't like they'd stocked liquor for their passengers. The captain had been clear his habit would not be supported.

Aren't sailors rationed grog? Surely there's rum somewhere aboard.

His stomach swam, but he kept down the bile this time. His vomit from earlier in the day stank up the room. Were he sick at home, he could have called for the maid to clean it up, but there were no maids here. He'd have to ask one of the women below to help. Toss a shilling at her. Maybe another if it would be enough for her to throw her skirts over her head.

The screams below continued, but now he heard male voices, demanding to know what the problem was, was the ship leaking, had something come undone? He laughed to himself as the women described a giant rat, big as a dog, that had run between their bunks. He was sure it wouldn't be the last rat they'd see. The men scolded the women for waking them and presumably went back to sleep.

He looked at his round pocket watch; four o'clock in the morning. The reek of vomit was getting to him, and he opened the porthole to let the smell out. The stink of saltwater hit him in the face. He slammed the porthole shut and finished off the scotch. Curling up in the rough blanket he'd found in the berth, he tried to find sleep.

The creaking of the rigging, the moaning of the ship, the damn cold, the certainty there was no hope on the horizon. It was all too much. It was all their fault, and there was nothing he could do to escape this hell.

"Well…" he whispered to the dark. "*Almost* nothing."

2014: Taylor

Taylor stopped to read the sign while the rest of the group moved on. The people on the boat in costume were doing an excellent job of bringing *Star of India* to life for her. She read about the emigrants that had gone to New Zealand, spending three months trapped below deck in the berths. She stared into the eyes of the people in the slightly blurred picture wearing skirts and jackets. They weren't smiling, but no one smiled in the old photos. She thought about sneaking in to lie down in one of the berths the emigrants had slept in but didn't want to get into trouble. Standing on tiptoes, Taylor peeked into the little box they said was a toilet. She couldn't imagine sitting on the wooden bench so many others would've sat on. Sniffing, she imagined the faint smell of sewage, a ghost from the past.

Her fifth-grade class had moved a ways ahead, and she kept an eye on them as she went to one of the portholes.

Imagine this being the only light?

And she'd learned they had to keep them closed or a wave might come through, soaking everyone and everything. If she squinted, she could almost see what it had looked like—families laying on berths, trunks everywhere, a boy running by, while his older sister in long skirts chased after him.

Her class had left to step down the ladder to the deck below but hadn't missed her yet. Stepping up on her tip-toes, she peeked out of another porthole, catching sight of the B-39 submarine. Maybe they could go aboard the submarine too!

Out of the corner of her eye, a shadow formed, a black figure in a hat. It moved toward her and she froze, heart pounding. He didn't look like the other crew, not with his scraggly beard and an odd hat, like Abraham Lincoln had worn. He leaned close to her face, and she felt his stinky breath across her cheeks. "Get off my boat," he whispered before fading away.

"Taylor?" One of the moms, a blonde with dark red lipstick, had come back. "Come on, sweetie. You're going to get in trouble. You don't want to get lost. You need to stay with the group."

Taylor had just one thought as she followed her classmates down the ladder, *Cool.*

1875: McBarnett

"Oi, did you hear?" Mr. Matheson came up to John Griffins as John leaned over the ship's side, trying to get some fresh air.

So far, the passage to Port Lyttelton had been rough, with high waves and lots of fog. The only colors they'd seen were the gray horizon, the gray sky, the gray air, and the boat's brown. Even catching glimpses of Miss Buxton's red wool petticoat had grown stale. The foghorn had gone off most of the nights, warning passing ships of their approach, and they'd wearied of the noise keeping them awake.

"Hear what?"

"The one passenger, the one with the top hat in the saloon, Captain McBarnett? You know the one we never see? The one that got dragged aboard dripping, he was so drunk?" Mr. Matheson said.

"Aye."

"He took his life last night."

"Blimey. How? Jump overboard?" John asked.

"Slit his own throat. With his shaving razor." Mr. Matheson mimicked using a razor across his neck.

John rubbed his throat, nearly feeling the slice of the razor himself. "Why? We're only five days out."

"He ran out of scotch."

John nodded, understanding. "Aye. So he was in the horrors[1]?"

"Aye."

---

[1] *In the horrors refers to alcohol withdrawal where the person experiences headaches, nausea, tremors, increased anxiety, and hallucinations after drinking. (Euterpe, Diaries, Letters and Logs of the "Star of India as a British Emigrant Ship, page 64)*

"Terrible way to go."

One of the sailors walked by with two buckets of water. Mr. Matheson leaned forward to whisper, "They're washing the blood away with that. Wanna go see?"

What else was there to do?

Together the two men approached the saloon. Sure enough, blood, more blood than John had ever seen, was flowing out of the room McBarnett had slept in.

"Know the worst part?" Mr. Matheson whispered.

"There's worse?"

"He did it at night, and the bosun[2] found him," Mr. Matheson whispered, "So they stitched him up and put him back in his room. He woke and *ripped* out his stitches. Ripped them out himself. That did him in."

The body, wrapped in a bit of sailcloth covered in blood, was carried out by two sailors. The men took a few steps back. Several passengers had gathered around to see this spectacle, though it cast a grim tide upon the decks. The men took off their hats as the departed passed by.

"They'll hold him 'til the inquest," Matheson said, as the sailors lifted McBarnett into the hold. "Then they'll say some words and dump him overboard."

"Overboard?"

"Where else? It's not like they can bury him and we can't keep him aboard until we reach land."

"Blimey."

*Cockburn McBarnett, Esq., late Lieutenant 92nd High-
landers, was set to rest at sea in December of 1875.*

---

[2] *Bosun*: Boatswain. Senior officer of equipment and crew

1999: Jessica

Jessica rolled her neck and kicked off the uncomfortable shoes that went with a sailor's costume from the mid-eighteen hundreds. Dark breeches, a blue topcoat, and a rough white shirt completed the costume. She was exhausted. It was always at night after a long day of guiding dozens of children through time, she wondered why she did this. Why she gave up her days and nights to walk fifth-graders up and over *Star of India*? They'd been a challenging class too, the students refusing to pay attention, banging on the bell, playing with the rigging, and running up and down the decks. She didn't envy the teacher or parent chaperones tonight.

But for the majority of these programs, the children were wonderful. On this program too there were a few children who listened to what she said, who stared around the deck as she described what conditions were like for the emigrants going to New Zealand. She could see their wheels spinning as they imagined living for three months in the tiny berths with barely any hint of sunlight. These were the kids who looked out the small portholes and whose eyes grew large when she told them how the sailors had punished the emigrants for opening up the tiny windows. These kids wrinkled their noses when she described the stench of unwashed bodies, vomit, spoiled food, and raw sewage collecting in the corners of the deck. These were the ones who made the job incredible.

Jessica changed into yoga pants and a soft t-shirt. She settled into the bunk in the First Mate's Cabin. It wasn't too uncomfortable with a thick sleeping bag, a gel pillow, and several soft blankets, but it must have been horrible for the first-class passengers sleeping here on their voyages. She wiggled around, reflecting that despite the rumors a ghost haunted this cabin, she'd never noticed or felt anything. And she must have heard the story about the guy ripping out his stitches a dozen times. But knowing she slept in a place where a guy had committed suicide never bothered her.

She opened her book and read until she fell asleep.

She awakened slowly, feeling the blanket creep off her body. Jessica reached to grab it before it hit the deck, but her hand clutched at nothing. Suddenly, something whipped the blanket off her body, her bare toes completely exposed. She opened her eyes with a gasp.

A man with a beard and a top hat stood over her.

"Get out!" She tried to shout, but the words wouldn't move past the lump of fear in her throat.

She tried again, "Who are you?"

The man leaned closer. She didn't recognize him; he hadn't been with any of the parents. Had a homeless man got onto the boat? But the dark clothes, the hint of a white-collar, and a tie belied that. And what was with the top hat? Who was this man?

He leaned closer, and she smelled the alcohol on his breath. When his lips quirked in a cruel smile, she started screaming.

Authors Note:

The First Mate's Cabin where McBarnett took his life is one of the more active places aboard Star of India. *Multiple volunteers and staff members report feeling uncomfortable in that space.*

We know little about what caused McBarnett to be strong-armed and sent to New Zealand. In fact, when we dug into his family history, we found conflicting information about his officership. We can infer officials may have caught him robbing, embezzling, or in a compromising situation with a woman or even a man. There's also the chance he was a pedophile or murdered someone. No matter what he did, his family was either trying to prevent a scandal or minimize it. We can confirm they paid for his ticket and sent him away.

And Captain McBarnett never left Star of India.

A Mysterious Connection

One of the more fascinating things about Captain McBarnett's story is that he's not the only person on Star of India *who tried to commit suicide by slashing his own throat. In researching this book, we found a mention of a cannery hand named Ramirez who, in 1918, also sliced his throat, "from ear to ear with a straight-edged razor". The surgeon aboard stitched him back up and the next day he "became violent and ripped out...the stitches."[3] They sewed him back up, after tying him down, and it is believed he survived, but the subsequent events are not listed on the logs.*

It is fascinating that two men aboard Star of India *sliced their throats AND ripped out the stitches. Were conditions so deplorable despite the approximate 50-year interval between both incidents? Or did both men suffer from untreated and undiagnosed mental health issues? And why the dramatic method of suicide? Why not jump overboard?*

If you know more about these stories, please let us know, as we would be honored to help bring their stories to life.

---

[3] *Star of India:* The Log of an Iron Ship by Jerry MacMullen, page 64

Lost Aloft: Johnny

1884: Johnny

The *Canadian* jerked violently, and a sound like a sea monster trying to break through the hull echoed through the deck. Johnny, Tim, and the other rats ran to the portholes.

"Blimey! There's 'nother boat out there," Tim said. "Think we hit 'em." He moved to another porthole. "Yep. Definitely hit 'em."

Another boat? This was his chance. Yeah, his mam, brothers, and sisters needed him to send back money, and he was going to do it. But this boat with its sailors who stole his food and pushed him down into the seawater muck accumulating in the corners of the deck wasn't where he should be. This was not where he belonged. *Euterpe*, now, with her towering masts and billowing sails, *there* was a vessel.

If their vessel were undamaged, the steamer *Canadian* would continue to London as planned. But what was waiting for Johnny in London? A cousin he had never met before? The prospect of joining him to be a tosher sounded worse than starving.

"They're saying up top that *Euterpe* is bound for New Zealand," Tim reported, running down the ladder where he'd been eavesdropping on the sailors.

New Zealand? Johnny thought. That was an adventure on the other side of the world. He didn't know anyone that had been there. He didn't even know where it was.

Imagine unclaimed land. I could be a farmer. The best farmer with the biggest potatoes anyone had ever seen. I could ride horses, kill deer, bring food home for a full belly, and no one would care. I could be the mayor of a town named after me, if I really wanted.

He had to go. He had to see New Zealand.

To do that, he had to get aboard *Euterpe*. Now. Before he lost the chance.

While the officers aboard the two ships talked to each other, their two boats bound together with lines as they determined their mutual damages, Johnny thought. He had to figure out a way to sneak aboard.

He eyed the portholes; he could see straight inside the other boat. Saw plenty of ropes, sails, and boxes to hide among. No one would know he was in there. The portholes between the two ships were lined up enough, and it was only a few feet away.

"You're not going to make it," Tim said. With tallow smeared across his clothes, this rat had stolen Johnny's rations of stale bread for the last time. "You're gonna fall, gonna get squished between the ships, gonna drown. And no one will jump in to save you. Think they care 'bout someone like you? Like us? We're nothin."

Johnny ignored him. *I promised my mam I'd make it, I'd find a better life. Not gonna find no better life in a sewer. I'm gonna make it. I have to make it.*

Opening the porthole on *Candian* perfectly lined up with the open porthole on *Euterpe*, he pulled his slender body up and out through the porthole. He kept his balance in the small rounded window on the underside of his thigh. His hand latched onto the top of the hole as he attempted to position himself for the jump.

The ship rocked up. The waters between the two vessels, his own of wood and the other of iron, made guttural glomping noises that sounded like an ocean monster belching.

Johnny swallowed hard. The macrame fenders did well to protect the ships' hulls from damaging one another any further but would do nothing for him.

"Go on then," Tim dared, pushing hard on Johnny's leg.

"Stop it," Johnny demanded. The perch he had in the porthole was no better than a large bird on a twig.

Johnny looked back to *Euterpe*. She rode the swell up, and then, upon her sweep back down, he leaped.

2014: Sarah

Dressed in outfits fashionable of the last century, dark breeches and thick peacoats, three educators sat around the rectangular table in Star of India's first-class saloon. Light filtered in the glass from the skylight above them, original and unbroken from the day the ship designers had placed it. But they focused on their phones, caught in the modern world's demands on their time. Aside from their breaths and the occasional swipes they'd make on their phones, all was silent and still. The subtle rocking of the iron-hulled vessel went unnoticed by the educators.

Sarah sat at the port side of the table, her feet tucked comfortably beneath the bench. They'd just received word the students were running forty minutes late, and she was grateful.

This was only her second time as an instructor aboard *Star of India,* and she had extra time to review what she would say to the students. She put her phone away and pulled out her black-bound notebook from under the tricorn hat she'd set atop the bench. While flipping through the pages, Sarah looked up at the other instructors in the room.

Rob, his curly dark hair overflowing from under his own black tricorn cap, leaned over the table, reading an Anime writer's interview on his phone. Luke, her other colleague, lounged on the settee, his head against the long mirror, his cap covering his eyes like he was tucking in for a nap. She wondered how many other sailors in the past had leaned like that against the settee, hat over their eyes for a rest.

She returned her gaze to her journal and read the rotation schedule for what felt like the tenth time that day.

A rounded toe of a boot kicked the instep of her tucked-back feet.

Sarah sat up, her eyes shooting forward. No one was there. Her companions were as they had been, Rob leaning over his phone, Luke lounging with eyes closed.

The kick had to come from someone behind her.

She turned her gaze to the mirror on her left, feeling like she was moving underwater. There was no one there. At least, no one she could see.

She couldn't have imagined it. Her entire body had moved from the impact.

Sarah pulled her feet forward and flat on the wooden planks. She swallowed hard then tried to communicate to the spirit that had just kicked her.

"Johnny, I don't have time to play. I have to get ready for this education program," she whispered. Waiting for a response, a

26

flicker of movement, sensation or even correspondence seemed like an eternity.

Nothing. But she was sure of all the spirits on the ship, Johnny had just made contact.

The Saloon looking toward the First Mate's Cabin

1884: Johnny

"Here he is, cap'n," the big burly man smelling of cheap tobacco threw Johnny to the deck of the saloon.

Ouch!

He'd hit the deck hard, and his shoulder smarted. Black boots stepped toward him. Johnny slowly looked up to the figure of the captain. The man's crown cap shadowed the other man's face, but Johnny felt the dark eyes boring into him. "So you're the stowaway, hunh?"

Johnny gulped and nodded.

"Answer him, boy." The sailor nudged Johnny with the toe of his boot, just a little less than a kick.

"Yessir," Johnny said, barely above a whisper.

"That's yes, Cap'n sir!" Now it was a kick to Johnny's side.

"Yes, Cap'n sir," Johnny yelped.

The captain crossed his hands behind his back and glared at Johnny a minute longer. The breath of time felt like years to Johnny.

"Now, lad, this is a voyage to New Zealand taking paying passengers to their destination," the captain started. "The people aboard poured their blood, sweat, and tears to be able to afford this passage. And my crew, these men have been hand-selected by me to pour their blood, sweat, and salt into seeing those passengers safely to port. You with me so far?"

"Y-yes, cap'n, sir." Johnny stuttered.

"We only have enough food aboard for those who paid or for those who are paid. So lad, where does that leave you?"

"As food for the rats," the smelly sailor growled.

Johnny began to shake. *I should'na jumped aboard.*

1977: Doug

On the days when foot traffic from visitors was slow, Doug would sit in a four-post wooden chair. The chair was clunky, but it sat heavily on the middeck, unlike the other chairs with wheels that slid whenever the ship rocked.

Doug lounged, his legs up on the gift shop counter, and gazed across *Star's* long-empty middeck, save for the various exhibits on deck. Affirming that he was alone, he turned back to his eleventh-grade history book to keep whittling away at his homework.

A squeak drew his attention from the pages.

"Hello?" Doug called, but the sound was far too close to be made from anybody stepping aboard or sneaking about his deck.

A slight movement to his left caught his eye.

It was the brass, spring-loaded clasp that kept the gift shop drawers with their goodies inside from opening with the waves' movement. The clasp was turning.

On. Its. Own.

Doug ripped his legs from the top of the counter and planted them hard atop the deck. He clutched his history book to his chest as if it was his shield against this invisible force. There was no way the movement of the ship could cause this. Opening the clasps was hard and required dexterity. A young child or an older adult with arthritis would struggle.

The clasp reached the end of its track and paused. His heart in his chest, Doug waited to see what would happen next.

The drawer opened.

Doug shook his head. He looked up to the lanterns decorating the gift shop. None were moving. Had the ship been rocking, those lamps would have been swinging.

He looked back to the drawer. It was now as open as far as it could go without falling to the deck, spilling its bright treasures within.

Sweat dripped down the back of Doug's neck. He'd been told ghosts haunted the ship and even heard the footsteps they'd said were from the *Euterpe's* first captain. But this wasn't a harmless ghost walking back and forth. This was an entity deliberately opening the drawer.

The drawer remained open for what felt like hours, and then just as slowly as it opened, it creaked close. Doug stared as the latch slid into place with a sharp click.

He jumped up from the chair, leaped over the counter, and clambered up the ladder, still clutching his history book.

He was clearly not alone.

1884: Johnny

Johnny cowered at the captain's feet, his side smarting from the kicks. What was going to happen to him? Why had he been so stupid to think they wouldn't find him?

The captain began to pace. He went back and forth two times before snapping his fingers. "I could feed you to the rats. I could also have you shackled and throw you below for the duration of the voyage." He paused, and bile rose in Johnny's throat. "But, it is my understanding our ol' cook could use an extra set of hands." He raised a brow at Johnny.

What's he saying? The cook will bake my hands? Or put them in the stew?

"How's it sound, lad?" The captain asked. "Pull your weight helping our cook or be thrown overboard? What do you say?"

"Yes, sir. Yes, cap'n sir, I could help your cook, cap'n sir." He felt like he could fly. He was going to make it to New Zealand! And be crew aboard *Euterpe*!

The captain inhaled deeply then pointed a finger at the boy. "It's not going to be easy work, lad. And if you so much as think about slacking off or skylarking, Cook will tell me. Understood?"

"Yes, cap'n sir."

"Now, pledge your blood, sweat, and salt to it, lad."

Johnny folded his hands over his heart as if in prayer and said, "I pledge my blood, sweat, and salt to it, cap'n sir."

The captain's lips twitched, and then he said, "Good lad. Mr. Paterson, take uh…"

"Johnny Campbell, cap'n sir," the lad informed.

"Take our young Mr. Campbell back to meet Cook."

1999: Stella

"You need to do something about the kids aboard this ship!"

Stella looked up from the list she tallied. She enjoyed being a docent, prepared to answer questions from tourists about *Star of India* and her history. But some tourists thought they could treat the docents like they were nothing.

"Excuse me?" Stella asked.

The sightseer speaking to her was an older woman, wearing a fanny pack, a pink baseball hat, and a "Pixie Dust and Churros" t-shirt. She was one of "those" tourists, the ones that came for the fun of places like the Zoo and beaches, but wanted to tell their friends they'd toured "cultural" businesses too. Well, it didn't matter, as long as they paid the ticket fees.

"There are children playing practical jokes on this ship, and I can't believe their parents let them do it. You need to tell those parents to keep their kids under control. I mean, how dare they harass me!"

Stella raised her eyebrows. "I'm so sor—" but the woman flounced off, her heavy footsteps practically rocking the gangway back to the pier.

Well, that was weird. She hadn't remembered seeing any kids come aboard; they generally didn't while school was in session, but maybe she'd missed them.

She moved to the main deck, standing in front of the saloon and running through her list of facts about *Star of India* and *Euterpe*. It was a perfect day on the San Diego Bay, the sun bright enough she had to squint against the glare on the water. But it warmed her shoulders and helped fight off the chill from the breeze. The other boats from the Maritime Museum floated around her as tourists went aboard each one. She looked toward *Berkely*, seeing the multi-colored heads bobbing along the deck and knowing they'd be upon her soon.

Some days as a docent were super busy as she explained what life had been like in all the ship's incarnations. But other days, like this one, were boring.

A couple came from below deck, holding hands. Stella smiled. She liked seeing couples still enjoying each other's company. But her smile faded as the pair kept looking behind them like something had spooked them. Maybe they'd fallen or gotten bruised going up and down the ladders.

"Excuse me." Stella went over to them. "Can I answer any questions about *Star of India* for you?" Up close, the woman was pale, her eyes wide.

"I think we're good," the gentleman said while the woman drew her green-patterned scarf closer around herself, her fingers trembling a little. "But thank you."

"I'm so sorry, "Stella pressed. "But I have to ask. Did something happen? Are you both all right?"

"We're fine," the gentleman said. He ran his fingers across the scrabble of a beard. "I'm sure it was nothing. We just…felt something on our backs, but I'm sure there was an explanation."

"Something on your back?"

The gentleman turned to his wife, who now looked like she couldn't wait to get off the ship. "Just a kid or someone playing a prank. And it was dark and shadowy down there. That's all it was," he said firmly. The woman shook her head, took his hand, and led him off the ship, all without looking at Stella.

Okay, something's going on. She left her post and went below, walking all the decks back and forth. She knocked on the heads and ensured all the random storage areas were not only locked but no one was hiding in them.

She couldn't find anything amiss. Just a few tourists walking between the exhibits, murmuring among themselves. No children.

Strange.

Stella returned to her post in front of the saloon, watching the people coming up from below, making eye contact and smiling at them, in case they had anything they needed to tell her. Several people came and went, and no one seemed spooked, so Stella relaxed.

But she was nearly at the end of the shift when a college kid came up from below. She met his eyes and smiled, inviting him to ask any questions. Sure enough, the young man came over. He was probably a history major or a writer, and those conversations were always interesting.

"I just had the most fascinating experience," he said. He shifted a notebook from hand to hand. "Some...one kept tracing an S on my back when I was below deck."

"An S? On your back?"

"Yeah and I kept spinning around, trying to catch who it was, and there was no one there. Do you know if this boat's haunted?"

Stella had heard the stories but never believed them. There was a rational explanation for everything, even this. But three people in one day complaining about something touching their back? Tracing an S, which was so incredibly specific. It wasn't possible.

"There have been lots of stories," she said. "But I've never heard of anyone complaining about an S traced on their back."

"Might be something to look at," he said, pushing his glasses up his nose. "Maybe people just think someone is playing a prank on them."

"And you're sure there was no one there?" Stella asked.

"Positive." The young man smiled at her and left, probably for a bar to tell his story to his friends.

This is ridiculous. There had to be a logical explanation. She went through *Star* again, not finding anything that didn't belong. No teenagers hiding behind barrels. No school kids left behind, hiding behind the exhibits of ship models. No bored families who really wanted to go to the San Diego Zoo, but someone had dragged them here. No teenagers looking for a quiet spot to make out or hang out with their friends and play pranks.

Maybe one of the volunteers was playing a joke on some of the tourists. After a quick reevaluation of who was aboard, Stella deduced none of them would upset the tourists. Jokes on each other were fair game, but not the visitors.

Stella went home that night, never having solved the mystery.

But later that evening, she read a book about the Victorian period that detailed playground games children would play. Out of the descriptions of hoops to chase with a stick, hopscotch to draw, and charades to perform was a note about playing tag and drawing a question mark on people's back. The school children were supposed to guess who had drawn it. If they were wrong, they were "it".

Had the tourists misinterpreted the question mark as an S? And who had done it? Had one of the ghosts been playing with the tourists?

Author's Note

The story presented to us was that "Stella" learned Victorian Children played tag by tracing a question mark on each other's back. Though we found many versions of tag, we could find none that mentioned a question mark or an "S" shape traced on people's backs. If you know more, we'd love to hear from you!

1884: Johnny

The blood, sweat, and salt Johnny gave to ol' *Euterpe* was the best investment the captain ever made. Every day, Captain Hoyle heard glowing stories about this young stowaway helping everyone he could on top of giving his all to his duties in the galley.

"No matter how hard we work him, he's always got a smile," the cook told the captain after giving his daily report on available rations. "He just wants to help in any and every way he can."

The compliments about Johnny came to the captain from

every way the wind blew. The passengers expressed how grateful they were for his bright smile below decks, and various lads on crew shared how impressed they were to see such a hardworking young man. The compliment that sang the loudest came from Mr. Paterson, who suggested, "Can we see how well he does hauling lines and joining our lads on deck?"

Making the stowaway crew was quite the story, one Captain Hoyle was happy to write. Before the table in the main saloon, the captain pulled Johnny over to his side. Stroking the length of his mustache, the captain asked, "Well, lad, tell me, are you liking it aboard?"

Johnny's head nodded up and down so fast that the boy's whole body moved. "Yes, cap'n sir. I love it."

The captain nodded slowly. Leaning back in his chair, he asked, "How might you feel, lad, about leaving Cook and joining the lads aloft?"

The boy's eyes doubled in size. "Aloft, cap'n sir?" He had heard the term before, but it seemed extraordinary to imagine that the captain would ask this. "Like, proper crew, cap'n sir?"

Nodding again, the captain answered, "Yes, lad. Would you like to be a part of our deck crew? Hauling lines and raising sails?"

Johnny wanted to jump up and down from his excitement. Instead, he sucked in his stomach and stood tall. "Yessir, cap'n sir. I'd be honored to, cap'n sir!"

Clapping his hands, the captain motioned to Mr. Paterson, who joined them. "Make it so, Mr. Paterson. See to it our young Mr. Campbell here knows every line and belaying pin by sundown tomorrow."

"Aye cap'n." Mr. Paterson motioned for Johnny to follow him, but Johnny cleared his throat.

"With all due respect, cap'n sir, Mr. Paterson, I already know 'em," Johnny informed him.

The two men looked at one another with raised brows.

"I don't doubt you, Mr. Campbell," the captain nodded his head and then said, "Let's just be sure, lad. It can get a little tricky when you're thirty meters or more above deck."

Johnny smiled. "Yes, cap'n sir."

Mr. Paterson patted the boy's head. "C'm along you. I do swear it won't be long before you put me out of the job, you will."

2017: Sarah

The sun shone like diamonds upon the water of the San Diego Bay. The reflection of the light danced throughout Sarah's office. Though she was used to the fine weather of her home city, today was extraordinary, the air crisp and fresh from a recent storm. It was much too fine a day to spend her entire time cooped up below decks in her office aboard *Berkeley*. Looking at her watch, Sarah decided she could spare a little morning walk to *Star of India*.

She bounded up the ladder across from the ferry boat's galley and headed out the back gangway, her keys on her belt providing a pleasant jingle in the morning. A crisp breeze rolled off the bay and filled her lungs. The waters were still, and only the crew moved about the museum. The gate would open at nine, in about ten minutes, which would give Sarah plenty of time to walk to *Star* and back.

She waved to Drew, getting ready for the tourists, as she passed by the ticket booth. Tide was high today and had pushed *Star of India's* ramp up to a dramatic angle.

Getting an excellent workout in, Sarah thought as she ascended.

The light touches of the morning were all over *Star.* Dew clung to her bulwarks, and a cool breath of night still lingered above her decks. All was still. Unusually so. Normally, by this time of morning, the ship was alive with students preparing to disembark after spending the night aboard in an educational program.

Lucky me, I have the whole ship to myself.

Sarah walked around the main deck, the sound of her keys on her belt disturbing the quiet morning air. She leaned on a railing, taking in the San Diego Bay as the sun rose and the day began. Around her, the boats of the Maritime Museum, the ferry boat *Berkeley,* the Soviet Submarine, the frigate *Surprise,* and the rest of the fleet were shaking off their nighttime doldrums and getting ready for the tourists.

Sarah took another peek at her watch. She only had time for a quick check of the decks before she had to be back for a meeting on *Berkeley.* Before stepping into the saloon, Sarah shut her eyes and thought as she approached, "Permission to enter." She didn't know if it did any good telling the ghosts aboard she meant them no harm or if it was just ludicrous paranoia. But she always thought the saloon felt lighter when she performed this ceremony.

The saloon was beautiful at this time of the morning. Light spilled in from the skylight above, shining on the table hundreds of officers and first-class passengers had eaten and made plans for the future on.

She decided to stop in the restroom before heading out. This room, the head, wasn't original to *Star of India,* and she breathed a quick thanks for that. She couldn't imagine using the chamber pot or the bucket those aboard had used in the past.

Once she was done, Sarah left the saloon, pausing to look up to the glorious stained glass image of *Euterpe* herself, smiling down from above.

Stepping back out onto the main deck, Sarah walked onto the ramp, double-timing it across the wood. It was time to get back to work.

However, halfway down the ramp, she realized that the silence had gotten...deeper. A sound was missing.

She closed her eyes, focusing. She heard the slap of the waves on the *Star's* hull, the sound of cars, of joggers running by, of tourists and their kids starting their day.

Sarah's feet stopped. She slapped her hand to her hip.

Where are my keys?

Turning slowly, she looked back to the ship. The second she faced *Star*, she whispered, "Johnny, I don't have time to play."

Heading back up the ramp, Sarah dismissed the thought. *Okay, think. I didn't hear them fall, and they're heavy enough to have banged on the deck. I know I had them. I heard them when I was walking on the deck.*

Retracing her steps, she reentered the saloon, repeating her request to enter, as she always did.

She stared down at the worn boards, looking for a glint of metal. Nothing.

Where are they? Maybe they're in the head? But there's no way they would have hit the deck without me noticing.

Returning to the room, Sarah looked all over the painted grey deck.

Nothing.

Where did they go? Did they fall into the toilet and I accidentally flushed them? No. There's no way.

She looked behind the commode, nothing. She looked around

the sink. Maybe she'd unclipped them from her belt and then put them down when washing her hands? It was ridiculous, and she didn't remember doing it, but…maybe?

Nope.

In desperation, she searched every corner and was about to give up when, on the farthest spot to the left, beneath the towel dispenser and hidden by a hanging towel were her keys.

She stared at them.

How did they get there? There's no way I would have taken my keys off my belt and thrown them way over there without remembering.

She extended her hand to reach for them. Taking the metal in her fingers, she looked at the black carabiner she usually hooked her keys on. It had never unhooked on its own. Her keys had never fallen off of her belt, nor would they ever again.

She laughed, wondering if Johnny was laughing too, feeling in her heart that her unseen friend had just pranked her.

1884: Johnny

He'd never climbed a tree before in his life. The highest he had been above the earth was when he jumped from the *Canadian* to this iron-hulled beauty.

Now, a hundred feet above the deck, laying out on the topgallant[4] yard, Johnny peered out to the endless glimmering sea surrounding his ship. The sun-speckled the waters with a million glittering gems, and the people below looked so small compared to it all.

He inhaled deeply, drinking in the breeze and feeling the presence of a world so much greater than him. He'd never felt

---

4 "Topgallant" pronounced, "t'gallant."

more connected to the ocean, to the earth itself. It was glorious, it was beautiful, and as *Euterpe's* newest crew member, it was all his. The most incredible adventure of any stowaway was his.

2016: Demi

Demi hunched her shoulders against the rain and cold. The ticket booth she worked in was cold in the winter, leaked in the rain, and was boiling in the summer. She wished she could just go home; no one was going to want to tour the ships in the showering rain. San Diego practically shut down when it rained. But she'd lose the hours and needed the money. She'd have to tough it out.

The phone in the booth rang, and Demi sighed. She picked up to listen to the event director asking for her help.

There was an event tonight aboard *Star of India,* and they had to dry out the decks; the museum would pay her double-time since she'd have to stay late. Closing up the ticket stand, she met the director aboard *Star.* He led Demi around the vessel, explaining the various areas where she needed to mop up the water, starting on the poop deck. When she was alone, Demi popped in her headphones and began to jam out to techno while mopping.

A tug on the back of her hoodie interrupted her music. She turned around and pulled out her headphones, but no one was there. Demi's brows furrowed.

"Hello?" she called, even though she was the only one on the deck. She looked at her earbud. *No answers there.* She turned her music off and tucked the earbuds back into her hoodie's pouch.

Demi went back to mopping in silence.

42

Another tug. Stronger this time.

Demi whipped around.

No one.

Authors Note:

On Thursday, June 26th, 1884, Johnny was on the highest mast "clearing the gear" and fell. He struck multiple yards before hitting the deck and fracturing both his legs. Johnny did not regain consciousness and lingered until late Sunday, June 29th. His body was wrapped in sailcloth and committed to the deep. The notes made in the logs by Captain George Hoyle and William Paterson, first officer, detailing whether or not Johnny could take broth, noting that everything was being done and their hopes he would recover are heartbreaking. It's easy to infer these men greatly liked and respected Johnny.

As we collected the ghost stories for this book, we found the majority attributed to Johnny. Many volunteers attribute anything unusual to him and, like Sarah, often speak to him, though he doesn't generally answer verbally. We believe Johnny is what's known as an intelligent or sentient spirit. Spirits like these are usually rare, and it's unusual to see one this active. Johnny likely knows he's dead and enjoys interacting with the living. He's unique as he tries to help most of the living he encounters, though he enjoys teasing regulars like Sarah and Demi. But there's never any fear or terror associated with his interactions. Most people report a feeling of playfulness, helpfulness, or mischievousness when Johnny does anything. In the introduction of this book, he's credited with helping Demi with the trash bags.

A medium aboard Star of India *once reported seeing a boy who sat with the other students to listen to stories about himself. She said those stories were his favorite, and he looked forward to hearing them over and over. There are no reports of Johnny frightening the children who have toured or spent the night aboard* Star of India. *He may view children as hands-off, preferring to spend his time helping and teasing the adults who volunteer and work aboard* Star of India. *Either way, he's a fascinating soul lost aboard* Star of India.

The Bell of Euterpe

It's terribly bad luck to change the name of a bell, though the ship's name and crew may come and go.

Lost to a Mutiny: Captain Storry

1864: Captain Storry

Captain Storry's head ached like there was an anvil banging inside his skull. He wanted another cup of coffee; anything to fight the heaviness pulling at his arms and legs. But it wouldn't do for the captain, a few days into the leg of their first journey, to work down the rations so early. It was one cup of coffee a day, and he had to live on that, just like the rest of his crew.

He paced the poop deck, his boots loud on the virgin planks. Over time, the sun, saltwater, wind, and rain would test this wood; the elements would bite down upon them, though his crew would do their best to maintain it. For now, this new ship was pristine and filled with hope for good journeys ahead.

Though exhausted, Captain Storry was thrilled to be the first master taking this iron-hulled, full-rigged ship to the seas. *Euterpe's* investors had entrusted him with the boat and her maiden voyage from Liverpool to Calcutta. His thoughts landed on the embarkation four days before. It had gone perfectly, better than expected, and *Euterpe* had pulled out of Liverpool to the cheers of those on the docks. He'd made eye contact with the investors and seen their relief as their gorgeous investment set to sea. Now he just had to get *Euterpe* to Calcutta in one piece.

Ellis hurried past him, coiling one of the lines on the deck without being asked.

"Good man," he told the green-eyed sailor. The seaman responded with a nod, and Storry noted how easily the lad had taken to life aboard the ship. Dealing with four-hour watch rotations late into the night, eating hardtack, laying out on the yards, and surviving the storms to come wouldn't be easy, but Ellis would be one to sign up again and again as crew.

Storry had a good crew, all hand-selected by him or his first and second mates, Sinclair and Dowd. There hadn't been any problems, but he couldn't resist the feeling of dread dogging his soul, the feeling that something was going to go wrong.

He walked the ship again, checking every chain, every rope, every nail, every barrel. The feeling that something was going to happen pulsed in his skull. He spoke to every sailor, every officer, checking with them, walking back and forth across the decks, climbing the ladders, making sure nothing would get missed.

Something is going to happen.

While death followed all ships, losing a sailor this early, even due to an accident, could curse their journey. He took a moment to remember the souls lost on ships he'd been aboard.

Storry returned to the helm and rubbed his head. The pain in his skull had intensified, his eyes grainy from the salt in the air and staring into the horizon.

Dowd heard the captain's boots on the deck long before he saw Storry coming toward him. "Rest," Dowd said, his cap pulled low against the sun glaring off the water. "It's a long journey, Captain. You can't stay awake the entire time. We're not due in Calcutta for six months." Dowd took a quick look at the binnacle (see Nautical and Paranormal Terms) before him, then returned his eyes forward over the long decks of *Euterpe*. "You have time."

Sleep did sound good, and Dowd was right. This was a long journey, and he needed to stay sharp. "Wake me at the first sign of any trouble."

"Aye, aye, captain. But there won't be any."

Captain Storry returned to his cabin below and lay down on his cabin sofa, knowing the discomfort of the piece of furniture would keep him from slipping into too deep a sleep. He toed off his boots but left the rest of his clothes on, just in case.

"Just in case of what?" he whispered to himself. The boat was sound, the crew tested and true. Nothing was going to happen.

* * *

The sound of Dowd calling a hail drifted into his dreams. Who was he hailing? It was probably nothing, but Storry pulled on his boots. The hails became more frantic, and the captain hastened out of his cabin, rushing out on the deck and climbing the ladder to the poop deck, two steps at a time. Night still held the seas, though the sky to the far east showed the faintest glow of dawn. How long had Dowd let him sleep?

More than half of his crew was standing along the starboard rail, waving their arms and shouting to the west.

A hole in the seas and stars stood thick and tall. Another vessel with her lights doused barreled down upon them.

Too close, too close, too close, his mind screamed.

"The hell are they doing?" he yelled. "Pull her hard over to port!"

The very figurehead of the approaching vessel seemed to be reaching out for *Euterpe*.

"She's hard over as she'll go, Captain Sir," Dowd reported.

The deck shifted, and a crash sounded, echoing through the hull.

A series of curses erupted from the crew.

The captain rushed to the forward rail of the poop deck, his eyes seeing the tangled mess of the ghost ship's jibboom with *Euterpe's* rigging.

"Sinclair, fetch Green, assess the damage, and take all hands to unfoul that blasted ship from us!" Captain Storry's voice sounded over the crews' clishmaclaver on *Euterpe* and the phantom vessel.

"Captain." Dowd rushed to Storry's side. "The ship had no running lights. We hailed her and directed her to pass astern. There was no answer."

"I can see that, Dowd." Storry muttered a curse under his breath and watched the other ship hang a red lantern. "Too late there, you fools!" he roared at the other boat.

They were four days from embarkation, and they'd collided with another ship. Was this what *Euterpe* had been trying to tell him?

Storry said, "Find out who that bloody captain is. And I want a damage report from Green in ten minutes."

He leaned over the side of the boat, seeing arms waving from the other brig. "Where is your captain?"

The men spoke at him. What language was that? Italian? Spanish?

"Dowd?" he roared.

"Aye, Captain?"

49

"Find me someone that speaks whatever language they're speaking."

"Aye, Captain."

The sound of the waves against the hull sounded odd to his ears, and he felt *Euterpe* leaning a degree toward port. "That list better be from them leaning upon us and not a bloody leak."

Someone shouted at him from the other vessel. Aside from "Captain," he couldn't understand a word of what they were saying. He wished he'd bothered to learn Latin.

"Captain?" The engineer Mr. Green approached him.

"What's the situation?"

Mr. Green stood tall and reported, "Our jibboom was carried away, the foresail, and the jibs are in tatters. And the headgear is fouled with their rigging and we're all tangled up. I'm not sure we'll be able to get them apart."

"Axes against their bow will do the trick, Mr. Green. Take all hands. I want every man on this. Doesn't look like their crew is in any hurry to get us apart. There's no leaks aboard then, I take it?"

"No leaks aboard, sir, but..." Mr. Green paused.

A wave of men from the other vessel jumped up to their bow. They sawed and hacked with a speed as if possessed. Within minutes, they freed their vessel and began to drift away.

"The devil is going on?" The captain watched as the other ship moved as if powered by steam. It was impossible to tell in the darkness that surrounded them. He'd never even gotten the name of the boat or the captain.

How on earth will I explain this to the investors?

Storry looked forward. His entire crew was busying themselves to right this mess. If they didn't get *Eurtepe* fixed, they'd be lost at sea. And his name would go down as the first and last captain of this ship. He wasn't going to let that happen.

"Mr. Green, no one sleeps until she's sound."

The sun would be rising soon, and his boots pounded the deck as he rolled up his sleeves to get to work with his crew.

1979: Bobbie

After a long day at school, the last thing Bobbie wanted to do after locking up was homework. But it was his job, and he was getting a room, rent-free, aboard *Star of India* for it. He turned off the lights in the bilge and circled the ship one more time. When he'd started this job, the odd corners full of ropes, boxes, sails had intrigued him and, if truth be told, made him uneasy at night.

Now they were old friends.

He dragged his feet across the deck and stopped to lean on a railing. Algebra could wait. The sun was setting in another spectacular San Diego evening, and the sky was alight with oranges, pinks, and purples. This truly was the best job he could ever have.

But as Bobbie's mom kept reminding him, he couldn't graduate high school without algebra, so he went to climb the ladder up to the main deck. If he just spent an hour, that would be enough time. Then he could read his comic books.

Heavy boot steps sounded ahead.

Bobbie's malaise vanished. *Now what?*

The museum was closed. No one beside him should have been aboard.

It was hardly the first time he would have to chase someone, probably homeless or drunk off *Star's* decks, but there was always a risk the person wouldn't go, would attack him, or be all drugged up.

And hell, all he wanted to do was curl up in his cabin in the saloon, read some comic books, and sleep. Now he'd have to chase someone off and maybe call the cops. And then he'd have to make a statement; he'd done it before.

Nothing else could've ruined the night more than this.

He ran up the ladder. The boots continued to clomp on the poop deck. "Hey!" He shouted as he rushed up the next ladder. "You can't be…" his voice waned as the deck came into view.

Where'd they go?

No one was up here. He turned his eyes up toward the rigging. Nothing but a web of lines looked back at him. He checked the backside of the companionway and still was alone.

The sound of bootsteps reappeared midship, 20 feet from his location.

What the…? How did that person get past me? Did I not hear it right?

Bobbie sprinted down the steps of the ladder, pursuing the man with the heavy steps pounding across his deck.

The moment his foot reached the main deck, the stomping stopped.

Bobbie raced across the planks, looking behind barrels, peering in the windows of the Sailmaker's Cabin and Cook's Cabin. But there was nothing. Just the sound of his own feet, the slap of waves on the ship, and the occasional whispers of the wind.

Bobbie's algebra homework would have to wait again.

1864: Captain Storry

"Cap'n!"

"Yes?" Storry looked up from studying the map in the aft Sailmaker's Cabin.

The crew was tired, he was tired, and the rations he was forcing them to maintain after such hard work hadn't helped. But the ship was sailable again. In the beginning, the crew had jumped to, cutting the befouled rigging and hammering new wood in place, but now they were worn and nursing sore muscles. He'd heard the crew's mutterings but couldn't do much about it, and it was a long way yet to Calcutta.

"Cap'n?" Ellis, the green-eyed seaman, said again. Storry shook the exhaustion from his head.

"Yes?"

"A moment of your time, Cap'n?"

"What is it, Mr. Ellis?" he asked. His instinct screamed at him to be cautious. He didn't like the look in the young sailor's eyes.

"The crew, sir..." Ellis started. He fiddled with his hat and shifted his eyes this way and that. "They want a word with you, sir."

Were Ellis and the crew demanding him to do something? He? The master of *Euterpe*?

"What would this word be about, Mr. Ellis?"

The man shifted his weight between his left and right foot. "Their concerns, Captain."

Captain Storry considered this a moment. He didn't like being ordered about by his crew, but it was time to confront this shadow of whispers head-on.

He followed Ellis to the main deck, where several of the crew waited for him. The sun had gone behind a cloud, and a chill wind blew out of the east. He put his hands on his hips and pulled down the brim on his hat. Did they think they were in control of this situation?

"Cap'n," Ellis started, his cap in his hands. "Sir, we the crew is requesting to put into the closest harbor immediately."

"Are ya now?" Storry's voice was soft, and several members of the crew stepped closer to hear him.

"Sir, the ship is not fit to continue at sea," Ellis continued. "We need a safe berth for repairs."

"I'll be the judge of what you need," Captain Storry reminded them. "Or did you forget the oath you took when you set foot aboard my ship? I see no reason repairs can't continue on the open sea."

Another seaman stepped forward, Fant, his skin tanned dark with sun and the sea. "With due respect, Cap'n, we'll do no more work 'til we're harbor bound. You can't force us."

"So it's a mutiny."

"No, Cap'n," Ellis stuttered, his green eyes finally meeting Captain Storry's. "But we will do no more work until conditions improve."

"I will take that under advisement." Storry realized this was not a grog-fueled attempt at mutiny. This was well thought out and discussed.

He ordered the other officers to meet him in the saloon.

"The crew is adamant, Captain," Dowd said. "They've laid down their tools and refused to work."

"Bloody, bunch of ingrates," Captain Storry muttered. "We'll do the rest of the work ourselves. And keelhaul the mutineers."

"I think it might be best to give in to their requests," Green said. "We are badly damaged, and a harbor would help ensure we can make repairs safely. There's been two broken arms since the crash. And it'll get worse before it gets better," he said. "The men are exhausted and becoming clumsy."

"I'm with Green," Dowd said. "It's best if we return to a harbor for repair. Anglesey Island is the closest with what we need for supplies and refueling."

"Are you all in agreement? "Storry asked.

"Aye," the other officers stated.

He did not like the idea of changing his word, but an unsettled crew, a crew not trusting his captain, was a matter he was not willing to endure for a week, let alone six months. There was a way to deal with this, and returning to port would accomplish that. And Anglesey Island was perfect. Holding his breath, Captain Storry said, "Then harbor it is."

The next morning, Storry ordered all of the crew above deck. "Seamen," he started. "Again, I ask, will you go on with the ship?"

"No Cap'n," Ellis said.

"So be it," Storry said. "We shall return to port for repairs." He smiled to himself as the crew shouted their victory. His team would learn the price to go against his wishes.

Two days later, they pulled into Anglesey Island. On land, Captain Storry called upon his good friends, the Masters Williams and Roberts. Over a healthy lunch, he outlined what he needed and told them the tale of the collision at sea.

They agreed though it cost him a hefty purse.

It would be worth it.

That evening, back on *Euterpe*, Storry called the crew above deck. Most came slowly, their eyes anywhere and everywhere but on him. But Ellis and Fant looked directly at him, contempt in their eyes. Gone were the shuffles, the "aye, aye captains".

Well, they'll learn.

He introduced Masters William and Roberts and fought to

keep the smile off his face as Masters Roberts unrolled a scroll. Holding it before him officially, Master Roberts read, "The following men are sentenced to fourteen days of hard labor for refusing to proceed to sea aboard the ship *Euterpe* bound on a voyage from Liverpool to Calcutta."

Captain Storry watched the faces, his gaze stern, of the seventeen men he'd named to Masters William and Roberts. The men's faces fell, and realization dawned. They'd never sail again. And Masters Williams and Roberts had assured Storry the fourteen days of hard labor would be the worst days of these men's lives.

Author's Note:

Captain Storry mastered only two voyages aboard Euterpe *and yet is one of the most legendary captains. He was a great captain by all accounts, though his journeys were full of strife and hardship. In addition to the collision and attempted mutiny,* Euterpe *almost sank in storms, forcing the crew to dispatch sails and cargo to keep her afloat. Despite that, it appears Captain Storry loved his time aboard* Euterpe. *His log is well written, and he seems to have enjoyed his crew, sailing, and the open waves.*

On August 8th, 1866, he died of remittent fever, which is a fever that fluctuates but never vanishes. It's common during heart infections caused by staph, or infections from ticks, fleas, lice, and mites. Insects such as lice were a common and significant problem on ships like Star of India.

Storry's not a very active spirit, but he is a repetitive one, and his heavy footsteps are heard frequently by volunteers and crew aboard Star of India. *Demi's story, in the introduction, is an example of that. There's some debate whether he's responsible for ordering visitors and staff to get off the ship, heard during various recordings and in oral traditions. However, these stories are generally accredited to an apparition wearing a top hat, and it's doubtful Storry wore one while aboard.*

Lost without a Name: "Chinyman"

Author's Note:

T his was a difficult piece to write, not only because this man's name was lost in time, but because it also exposes an ugly side to American history, specifically toward Chinese Immigrants. In researching this book, we found no names for any of the Chinese Immigrants aboard Star of India - literally, no one cared enough to write down their names in logbooks. These men came to the United States hoping and dreaming of a different future. Instead, they were abused, murdered, and delegitimized to the point their names and stories were lost.

By this point in history, Star of India had passed through many owners and been retrofitted as a fishing vessel, collecting her wares in Alaska's waters with the Alaskan Packers. Gone are the emigrants heading to New Zealand, the first-class passengers, and the trips around the world. It was a new century, and Star of India traveled between San Francisco and Alaska hunting for and delivering fish.

The fishermen aboard, called anglers, were all immigrants from various areas of the world. Sometimes as many as 300 people were crammed below deck in an area as large as six city buses. They would assemble with those from similar parts of the world. While *they worked hard during the day fishing, hauling nets, and preparing the fish for market and storage, the evenings were generally open. Reports of knife fights, gambling, drinking, and opium were standard upon ships like* Star of India.

The name given to this ghost was "Chinyman," but we will leave him unnamed for this publication. We do not mean any disrespect to his memory or his family, and it deeply saddens us that while oral tradition remembers the story of his death and his ghost remains on Star of India, *his name and journey aboard have been lost. We infer a great deal for this story, utilizing other Chinese immigrants' stories on* Star of India *and similar boats in the early 1900s. If you know more about this man, please contact us so we may tell his story more fully.*

1904

I climbed the stairs to the above decks, taking a breath of the clean ocean air. A storm was on the horizon; I saw the threat of ice and rain in the clouds ahead. Somehow, we'd missed its fury, and the storm fell behind our ship. I breathed deep, the cold air filling my lungs and pushing away the smell of the fish, unwashed bodies, and blood from below.

I hadn't realized so much blood could come out of a human body. The fight had been stupid, over a few mouthfuls of hardened meat Hai-Lun had stolen out of the kitchen. He'd been showing us his plunder, proud he'd been so sneaky and offering us an extra bite. We'd turned him down. No one wanted to take the chance of being caught. Somehow Burnes must have seen, though we'd been trying to keep it secret.

Burnes had walked behind Hai-Lun, grabbed him by the shoulder, yelled in his face, and then walked on. We didn't even know what had happened until Hai-Lun dropped to his knees and fell forward. The blood had leaked quickly, the metal tang sharp in the heavily fouled air of below. Someone said it was a stab to the kidney. We patched him up, and luckily, they let us put him into the Cook's Cabin where it was warmer. They'd said he might survive, might not.

I looked down; Hai-Lun's blood was still under my nails and staining my shirt. Burnes now owned Hai-Lun's things, including the stolen rations.

This was a different world than I'd envisioned. When I signed on, they'd said the fishing was good in Alaska, that there was money in the fish. Enough for my shop when we got back.

They'd been wrong. The catch had been paltry, they said, compared to earlier years. And it was cold. Damn cold. Ice floated past us, day in, day out, mornings and nights. We had to stand watch at all hours, our fingers turning blue, searching the waters for floating icebergs that could kill us, not fish to feed us.

I leaned on the deck railing, the new sun warm on my face. We'd be back in San Francisco before the ice froze us in, they told me. I hoped so. I hoped my share would be enough to bring my family to the United States. Daydreaming a bit, I thought about the general store my brother and I planned to open. I'd found the perfect place in Chinatown and couldn't wait to show my brother.

I straightened up as Captain Swanson moved across the deck. He'd recently shaven, enforcing the rule that the officers were clean-shaven, and a small drop of blood stood out on his neck. He greeted me, unsure of my name, only that I was one of the anglers. The captain was tough, but he was one of the only of the proper crew who looked at us with a lick of respect. To the rest of them, we were worth far less to them than the guts of the fish.

Perhaps I should tell him about Burnes, about the thieving and knife fights? Maybe he would care and do something about it.

I nodded back at him, greeting him with a "Good morning." My English was getting better, though I understood it much better than I spoke it.

The sun lit the ocean orange as it crested the horizon, and dolphins danced in the waves. Leaning over, I faintly heard their clicks as they lept above the waves playing in the wake from *Star of India*. I couldn't wait to get back to shore, but I'll miss mornings like this.

I heard the grunts of the men as they went to the cookhouse to get their morning breakfast. Joining them, I took my rations, chewing on what the other sailors called "hardtack." It was a tasteless clump of flour, so hard that it'd break your teeth if you tried to bite it, but something was better than nothing. Burnes, his skin brown from the sun glinting off the ice, came through, elbowing people out of line, taking half of their rations. We knew what would happen if we said anything after last night. I met the eyes of the other men like me, and we looked down, pretending we hadn't seen anything. Maybe that's why so many of the older anglers take to the pipe - to forget.

I'd ask the others tonight about going to the Captain. We had to do something. It was a long journey back to San Francisco.

After breakfast, Goodmand, one of the other anglers, told us we'd be raising anchor to head back to San Francisco. The crew cheered! Goodmand issued the orders, and I couldn't hide my smile. I'd be one of the men pulling up the anchor on the forward capstan. It was hard work in the cold air, but at least I was above deck in the light and away from the stink below.

As I climbed the ladder to the foc's'l[5], Burnes elbowed me in the gut. I tried not to double over, but my eyes watered with the pain. But I didn't stop and fought to get air past the iron band in my chest.

I joined the others, giving them a quick nod. I was the only man from China up here. Burnes made an angry slur about me and pulled his eyes rigid in the corner. They thought I couldn't understand, but I did.

Shouting at me like I was stupid, they ordered me below to stack the chain as they pulled up anchor. If we weren't careful with how the chain lay in the chain locker, it could get tangled and cause problems when we dropped anchor.

Frustrated, I did as they asked and descended into the dark deck below, directly below those men that sent me down here. Grabbing the pole, I leaned over the chain locker, using the cold metal pole to nudge the heavy links into position. I was careful not to look directly below me; it was a long fall down and one that would hurt.

Someone came up behind me. A fist struck the back of my head, and the world enclosed me in darkness.

---

[5] Foc's'l sailor word for "forecastle," pronounced, "folk-sul."

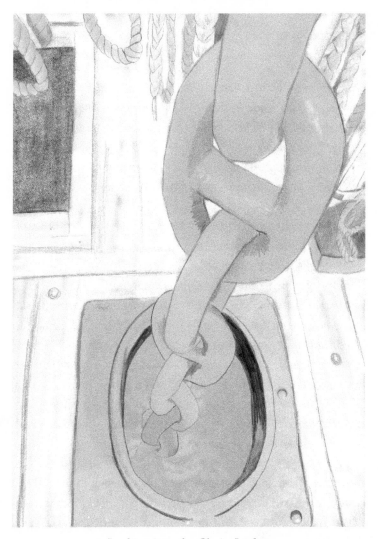

Looking into the Chain Locker

Author's Note:

As this story was passed down by oral tradition, accounts vary of what happened to this Chinese Immigrant. But somehow, while the crew raised the anchor, he fell or was caught in the chains. There's some debate about whether or not he was working, as no one should've been in the chain locker when the crew raised the anchor; it was too dangerous. Instead, crew members would lean over the chain locker with a long pole and ensure the chain links went into the correct place.

Legend tells that this man's body was found buried beneath thousands of pounds of anchor chains. Each link of the anchor chain weighs twenty-five pounds (see picture below). Though the links are extremely heavy, it is unlikely that the chains themselves were the cause of death for this man. In our retelling, we have implied that something far fouler was afoot. Conversely, some of the stories recounted to us regarding this spirit told of the opposite; that he was minding the chain as the anchor was dropping, got caught up in the chain, and was ripped up through a hole, severing his legs.

In doing our research, we only found a mention that a "Chinyman" died, and his body put to sea. While history has lost his name and the truth of his passing, his spirit lives on.

Many crew and visitors report cold spots in the areas where the links of chains reside, cold enough to produce goosebumps and shivers. Visitors who report this phenomenon generally do not know the story, as there's not much solid information for the staff to share. The cold spots do not appear to move and are on multiple decks where the chains feed. Staff report feelings of sadness, loss, and pain and generally do not like to be in these areas for very long. While this spirit is not one of the more active ghosts, he can almost always be found in the same spot by those sensitive enough to feel such things.

It's widely thought that Demi's experience with the lights turning on below deck belonged to the activity of this spirit. Perhaps he was trying to communicate or doesn't want to be alone in the dark with just the sound of the water slapping the bulkheads and the click of pistol shrimp beneath the ship. Maybe he was trying to get her to come below deck again. Demi's experience with the lights turning off and on is not unique, and other staff report similar issues with the lights below decks.

We hope that speaking of him, and keeping his story alive a little bit, provides this man some peace in the afterlife.

Size of a hand compared to one link in the chain.

Lost Below: Other Experiences

Authors' Note:

*T*here are phenomena and spooky encounters aboard Star
of India *we couldn't attribute to specific entities. Each of
the spirits we've written about so far has a historical person
attributed to them through the oral traditions, allowing us to do
research and draw some conclusions about what their life was like.
But the stories in this chapter are vague, and we couldn't in good
conscience assign them to the other ghosts we've discussed. Perhaps
there are more ghosts aboard, or there are nuances with the previously
mentioned ghosts we're not understanding. But either way, here are
some more stories from those souls lost aboard* Star of India.

2017: Allana

Allana grabbed for her phone, dropping it onto the wooden
deck beneath the berth she slept in. Those bloody parents from
the educational program were rooting around in the random
drawers of the Cook's Cabin! She'd been very clear with them
when she'd set out the hot chocolate and coffee what was off-
limits.

But waking to the sound of metal tinkling against metal could only be someone messing around in the drawers and cupboards of the galley on the opposite side of the bulkhead where she slept. Needing light, she cursed to herself as she felt for her phone. The sound came again, but she knew better than to bolt out of her sleeping bag into the historical ship without light. Fog from the Pacific Ocean covered the stars and moon, and it was so dark she could barely see the berth she slept in. The ship listed slightly in the waves, the slap of water loud in the darkness.

Her fingers finally closed on the plastic case, and she lifted the screen to her face. 3:34 a.m. Who on earth was up this time of the night? 2:00 a.m. on was a quiet time when the Night Watch tried to catch a few hours of sleep. By this point, the parents and kids spending the night on the ship had normally passed out from exhaustion.

She clicked on the flashlight icon of her phone, lighting up the white walls of the berth. During daylight, the windows and white walls made the old Cook's Cabin, the place where the cook for *Star of India* had slept, a pleasant-seeming place.

But nighttime was different.

The female staff members hated this room. It seemed like something watched them, something angry. To Allana, that feeling tonight was tough to shake off. But she didn't have a choice. As the cook in the educational program aboard *Star of India,* it just made sense to sleep in the cabin. Usually, she was exhausted enough after a full day of pretending to be a cook from the 1800s, showing the students how the cook used the space to prepare meals for all the sailors, then cooking dinner and preparing for breakfast, to ignore the feeling. Cook was one of those roles that was easy, but long.

The sound came again, but different. Now someone was running their fingers over the old kitchen utensils, the ladles, and giant stirring spoons hanging on the walls as props. She was going to kill those dads. And she knew which ones they were. The ones who had laughed at everything, the ones who pretended to push one of their kids overboard, the ones who kept saying the kids would be keelhauled if they didn't pay attention.

She'd known they'd be a problem.

The sound came again, the metal clanging louder. Someone was going through the drawers *and* rubbing up against the hanging utensils?

Ridiculous. Didn't these idiots realize we're on a floating museum? Didn't they have any respect?

Using the anger as a buffer, she swung her feet out of bed into flip-flops and zipped on a hoodie. She ignored the trembling in her fingers, telling herself it was from the cold ocean air pouring through the open windows.

She felt the invisible eyes tracking every move, every shake of her fingers.

She shook away the heebeegeebees feeling and went out into the kitchen area proper, where the old pots and pans and bits of "historical" equipment hung.

She'd expected to see the dads' moving silhouettes, to hear them shifting around the room as they rooted around for hot chocolate and coffee fixings. But there was nothing. The tools hanging on the wall were still, like nothing had actually touched them.

Allana gulped. "Hello?" she called into the darkness.

No sounds broke the stillness of the kitchen. No giggles from parents, no whispers breaking up the shadows. She could hear cars out on the highway beside the harbor where *Star of India* lived and the sound of the water slapping against the hull. But nothing else.

A sound came from behind her, the hanging ladles clanking. She spun to see them moving, swinging back and forth. Something they might do in a powerful storm, but not on the flat water of the San Diego Bay.

Queasiness rose in Allana's stomach.

Those damn parents had to be hiding in here somewhere. It *couldn't* be a ghost. There was one more place to look. The pantry. It was the only place that made sense since it was on the opposite side of her bunk's wall. Maybe they were punking her. Parents playing jokes on the educational team or the other way around was not unheard of.

In slow steps, Allana rounded the bulkhead behind the ancient oven. The pantry door was closed. They were probably in there now, silently giggling at her.

Okay, just open the door, and tell them to get out of there.

Allana held her breath. She reached for the door and pushed it open.

A dark room greeted her.

She shone the light from her phone, illuminating cans, boxes of food, and a tray of forks, knives, spoons. Everything was just as she'd left them.

A clink sounded from the stove, and she spun again. Had… had that heavy pot for the "rat stew" always been on that burner? She thought she'd left it on the counter, and she definitely hadn't left the top half hanging off.

"Hello?" She called again. She felt the unseen eyes of whatever was in the Cook's Cabin bore into her.

Heart pounding, she went back into the Cook's Cabin and

zipped into her sleeping bag. Unable to think about sleeping, she turned on a little light and played with her phone until the sun rose and the feeling of the entity faded away.

The Cook's Cabin

Author's Note:

The Cook's Cabin is an uncomfortable area of the ship, and we talked with several people who describe the feeling as if "someone is in there, watching them hungrily." As author Sarah explains, "I don't like being in there. It's just a weird feeling. It's not menacing; it just feels like someone is staring at you and wondering why you're in their bunk. As bright and as happy as it is in that cabin, it just feels like you're not alone in there."

Theresa overlooked the room's oppressiveness when she toured but noted how different the next room, the Sailmaker's Cabin felt. The Cook's Cabin is light and clean with open windows and white walls. Conversely, the Sailmaker's Cabin is dark and filled with odds and ends. But the Sailmaker's Cabin feels friendly, like when you're visiting an antique store full of interesting items. Your hands will get covered with dust, and your allergies will act up, but everything feels welcoming. The Cook's Cabin doesn't have that feeling. It feels... cruel.

* * *

Author's Note:

Spooky as those interactions may have been, there have been very positive moments with spirits as well. In 2017, long-time employee Captain John and author Sarah Faxon used divining rods, also called dowsing rods, or copper rods, to communicate with the spirits aboard. For the sake of the living relatives of the spirit they communicated with, we have changed that individual's name.

2017: John and Sarah

"Thanks to the ghost tours I've been leading in Balboa Park," Sarah said to her co-worker John and pointing to a white bucket in the back of her office. "I have some divining rods; maybe we can see if anyone will speak with us on *Star of India*."

"Do you think that would work?" John asked.

"Can't hurt to try. What's the worst that could happen?" Sarah asked, reconsidering it almost immediately, but also very excited by this opportunity.

The pair headed over to *Star of India*.

"Should we try below?" Sarah asked. On the walk over, she'd begun to consider all the terrible things that could happen if they contacted the wrong spirit. "Wait, I changed my mind. It's a little too spooky down there."

"How 'bout the First Mate's Cabin," John suggested. Something was drawing him there like one of the ships' lines pulling on his heart.

A different feeling filled Sarah. As long as she had worked there, people had told her the First Mate's Cabin was where the scary encounters occurred, which, given the cabin's history, more than made sense.

"Alright...I guess," she said, pushing down her doubts.

They pushed open the gate, then boarded the ol' iron-hulled ship. Stepping aboard the sleeping vessel, the quiet of morning greeted them. The street sounds of traffic and joggers running by, listening to their podcasts on earbuds seemed like a world away. They entered the saloon, Sarah shutting her eyes and repeating her ritual of silently asking permission to enter.

The cabin they sought was the first on the right; tiny, like the other first-class and officer's cabins, were. Nestled against the portside bulkhead, there was only room inside for a chair, a small desk, and a bunk, all huddled tightly together. John entered the cabin first and leaned against the side of the bunk.

Sarah didn't want to go in. The air felt heavy, oppressive. She stayed by the door, her instincts telling her to flee.

This no longer felt like a good idea.

Gulping hard, she handed John his pair of copper, L-shaped rods.

"Now remember," she started, feeling a tremor in her voice, "Hold the plastic on the smaller part so that they'll move easily. Place your thumb over the elbow of the copper wire. If the ghosts are here, if they want to talk, they'll move the stick, and this way, it won't just start swinging around on its own."

John and Sarah positioned the rods in their hands, Sarah wiping her sweaty palms on her jeans first.

"Hold them out in front of you." She bent her arms, so her elbows were at her side, her hands pointed straight out. "First question to ask is, show us your yes and no, so we know how it's going to answer. Then we'll start asking yes or no questions."

John took a deep breath.

The First Mate's Cabin pressed in around Sarah, and she felt like she had to swallow her pounding heart. This room had never felt like this to her before.

Looking up, John started, "Hello. Is there anyone here with us? If so, could you please move Sarah's or my copper rods and show us your no?"

Nothing happened.

A few seconds passed, and Sarah looked up to John as he said, "So if there's anyone here, how about showing us your yes?"

The silence continued, but, for Sarah, it intensified. The faint noises of streetcars, of the people talking as they passed by on

Embarcadero receded. Darkness crowded around her vision, and the tiny room seemed to shrink even further. Her breath shallowed, and a tingling sensation ran from her shoulder to her right hand.

The copper rod in her hand moved. It turned, pointing to the right, then stopped, the motion intentional, like a finger other than her own had been in control.

Sarah's stomach clenched. She looked at John. It felt like someone had stolen words and the sense of speech from her.

The tools in John's hands did not move. He placed his copper rods on the bed, seeing that the spirit was choosing to communicate through her.

Sarah tried to gulp, but her throat was so dry. She exhaled slowly then returned the rod to the center to await the next answer.

John was breathing quickly but said, "I guess that's a yes then. Um, first of all, thank you for speaking with us - we'd like to find out a bit more about you. Were you a passenger aboard?"

The rod did not move.

With a nod, John asked, "Were you a part of the crew?"

The tingling sensation returned to the top of Sarah's shoulder, the tiny fingers of electricity running down her arm and to the rod in her hand.

It moved to the left.

"Okay then." Eyes wide, staring at the copper rod, John wondered what to ask next.

Sarah didn't know what to expect as her knees started trembling, and it took an effort to keep her hands from shaking. She didn't like this idea that something she could not see was manipulating her energy to communicate.

"I guess we should start from the top then work our way

down?" John asked, but Sarah was unable to answer verbally. She nodded her head, then reset the copper rod. "Were you one of the captains?" John asked the spirit.

No feeling of electricity tickled to life in Sarah's arm and the rod did not change its position. She looked up to John, let out a breath, and shrugged.

"Were you the first mate?"

The electricity ran through her arm, and the copper rod turned to the left again.

John's forehead beaded with sweat, but he knew he had to continue. "Were you first mate when *Euterpe* was sailing to India?"

The rod did not change.

"How about when she was sailing to New Zealand?"

The feeling did not change in Sarah's arm, but a faint tingling told her the spirit was still with them.

"With Alaska Packers?"

Nothing.

John's brow furled. "What else is there?"

Sarah shook her head but remained silent.

Dropping his shoulders, John asked, his voice deep, "Were you a part of the restoration?"

The rod turned. The energy had run through Sarah's arm fast, like the spirit was excited to answer.

Pushing his lips to the side, John tried to think. "Who on earth would have worked on the restoration and called themselves the first mate?"

A feeling like a pair of hands pushing through her, a question came flying out from Sarah's lips, "Did you work with John?"

The energy burned through her arm, hotter and faster than any before.

75

The rod turned fast, pointing directly at John.

A name rose to his thoughts, one that he had not thought on in ages. "Walt? Walt Carson?"

The same burning energy coursed beneath her skin and turned the copper rod straight toward John.

Sarah and John's eyes were as wide as they ever had been. Sweat formed on Sarah's brow. John wiped the forming drops from his upper lip with shaking hands.

"Walt?" John asked again, his voice trembling.

Again, the surge of electricity and the rod moved to confirm.

John's eyes lined with tears. He looked at Sarah and said, "He was my first boss. The guy who hired me when I was a teen. He took a chance on me when no one else would." John snuffed, then said, "He left when I went away to school. I never got a chance to thank him for everything he did for me before he died."

"Thank him now, John," Sarah said, still holding the rods before her. "Thank him now."

John inhaled deeply. This was an opportunity he never imagined he would ever receive. "I'd always heard that after you left, Walt, you were disappointed in me for not leaving, for not doing more with my life, and I thank you for that thought, but I'm incredibly grateful. My life is happy. I'm proud to have made this a career. It's because of you that I not only got to work here for so long, I got my chief engineer license, I earned my captain's license. All this stuff that I would never have done, if you hadn't given me that shot, so…thank you, Walt. Thank you for believing in me."

John wiped his eyes. He looked away, then said, "I'm so glad that this is your home and that *Star* will always be safe with you aboard."

The sounds of the world beyond the iron hulls mulled back to life. The hum of downtown traffic, the footsteps of the walkers, and the voices of the tourists, their presence returned and light filled the cabin once more.

Walt had receded with other ghosts aboard *Star of India.*

Star of India's Legacy

Though a floating vessel, *Star of India* is one of the iconic pieces of San Diego's landscape. When I initially applied to work at the museum in early 2014, I mentioned I was never officially home from my university in New York until I saw *Star*. When I first started working at the museum, I thought it would be a winter job to hold me until I found something within my scope, which, at the time, was in international relations. What I instead found was a love and passion for the fleet that has truly become a part of me.

We often joke as employees that you can never truly leave once you become a part of the museum. The spirit of the vessels intertwine with our own. There is something particularly extraordinary about *Star of India*; whether it's her history, her trials, the events that have taken aboard in our lifetimes, she is a precious treasure we must continue to protect and preserve for future generations to enjoy. In writing this book, we hope that we have presented many of her legends to a new wave of adventurers and admirers who will help us in our quest.

If you haven't visited yet, the trip is well worth it. And, who knows, maybe while you're visiting, you'll also find someone who is lost aboard.

—*Sarah Faxon*

Euterpe's/Star of India's Timeline

- Jan 9, 1864: First voyage! *Euterpe* leaves Liverpool for Calcutta
- Jan 13, 1864: Collision and attempted mutiny
- Nov 15, 1864: Return to Liverpool
- Dec 31, 1864: Left London for India
- May 13, 1865: American Civil War Ends after 4 years (began in April 1861)
- Aug 8, 1866: Captain Storry dies of "remittent fever"
- Feb 3, 1870: 15th Amendment ratified, giving African American men the right to vote
- Oct 10, 1871: Great Chicago Fire destroys 17500 buildings and kills over 300 people
- Dec 23, 1871: Euterpe starts running emigrants to New Zealand until 1897
- Dec 20, 1875: McBarnett dies
- Aug 26, 1883: Krakatoa eruption
- Mar 27, 1884: First long-distance call Boston to New York
- Apr 9, 1884: *Euterpe* runs into a steamer named the *Canadian*
- Jun 26, 1884: Johnny dies from a fall from the tallest mast
- Feb 18, 1885: Adventures of Huckleberry Finn published

by Mark Twain
- May 8, 1886: First Coca-Cola sold. It was originally advertised as a non-alcoholic drink as temperance gains a foothold in the United States
- Jul 10, 1888: Voyage to South America
- Feb 16, 1896: First newspaper cartoon strip
- Apr 20, 1898: Went to Newcastle for Honolulu
- Aug 12, 1898: Hawaii becomes annexed, which was the first step to it becoming a territory (1900) and then a state (1958)
- Nov 2, 1899: Boxer Rebellion begins
- Jan 16, 1901: *Euterpe* sold to Alaskan Packers
- Summer 1901: Significant remodel to turn *Euterpe* into a fishing vessel
- Mar 18, 1902: Left San Francisco for Alaska
- May 6th, 1904: "Chinyman" dies
- Jul 20, 1905: Chinese boycott of 1905
- Jun 1906: Name changed to *Star of India*
- Jun 26, 1909: First commercial airplane sold for $7,500
- Apr 14, 1912: Titanic sinks after running into an iceberg
- Apr 18, 1918: Canneryhand Ramierez tries to commit suicide by slitting his own throat
- 1926: Bought by Zoological Society of San Diego for $9,000 for a planned museum and aquarium
- Jul 9, 1926: Brought from San Francisco to San Diego
- 1927: Gilbert and Sullivan's "Pinafore" performed onboard to raise money. When all the bills were paid, it raised $4.85 and was considered a waste of time and money
- Nov 23, 1959: Moved to dry dock for repairs
- Dec 28, 1959: Moved back to Embarcadero, where it remains as a museum

- 1975: *Star of India* restored
- Jul 4, 1976: *Star of India* sales with a volunteer crew
- Nov 2013: *Star of India* Celebrates 150 years of life at sea
- Nov 2018: *Star of India* sets sail to the open sea

Nautical and Paranormal Terms

We've included the following terms to help you on your nautical and paranormal journeys.

Nautical terms

Aft: The back or stern of the boat

At loose ends: The ends of lines flapping. Now it means nothing to do

Batten down the hatches: Prepare for trouble or lock down the hatches or trapdoors in the decks' ships

Bilge: the lowest point of a ship's inner hull

Binnacle: A housing for a ship's compass

Bosun: Boatswain. Senior office of equipment and crew

Bow: The front of the ship

By in large: References to looking at the big picture or looking at lots of things

Clishmaclaver: gossip

Cut and run: Moving quickly. In ship terms, this references when a ship would cut its anchor in emergencies to escape or move soon.

Dead in the water: Stopping, or getting stuck, or not going anywhere. Nowadays, you hear it regarding cars breaking down and not being drivable. In ship terms, it meant having no wind and not sailing anywhere. It may also refer to a badly damaged ship

Flogging: whipping

Footloose: Independence, often doing fun things instead of being responsible. This referred to the 'foot' of the mainsail not being adequately tied down and "loose"

Forward: The front of a ship

Give a wide berth: To avoid something. It references giving enough room for a ship to maneuver at a berth or when dropping anchor

Grog: Alcohol allowed on board. Depending on the time and the captain, this may have been carefully rationed and/or watered down

Hard and Fast: Beached ship. Today it means something that is direct and moving quickly, usually an event or a process

Hardtack: Dry bread or biscuits. Rations for long journeys at sea

Head: The bathroom or toilet on a ship. The name comes from the regular sailors' toilet being placed in the head or bow of the vessel

Helm: The tiller or wheel of a boat. A device used to steer the ship

Hull: The body or frame of the boat

In the Doldrums: Depressed and dull. In nautical terms, it references an area north of the equator with calm winds that make it hard for ships to sail through

Jib: A triangular sail ahead of the foremast

Jibboom: a spar used to extend the length of a bowsprit on sailing ships

Keel: Backbone of the ship running along the bottom of the boat from stern to stern

Keelhaul: A form of punishment consisting of dragging a sailor or passenger through the water under the keel of the ship

Let the cat out of the bag/Cat-of-nine-tails: Tell gossip or a secret. This refers to the 'whip' used during flogging. It would be kept in a bag and caused scratches similar to what an angry cat would cause

Mainsail: The sail on the main mast of the ship

No room to swing a cat or no room to swing a dead cat: Being in a tight space or a tight situation. This is another flogging situation when sailors would crowd on the deck to witness it

Over a barrel: Being in trouble, being manipulated into a situation you can't get out of. This referred to flogging sailors by tying them over a barrel and whipping them for infractions

Pipe down: Stop talking. This used to be part of a whistle sailors used to say it was time to go below-deck

Port: Left side of the ship

Rigging: System of ropes, pulleys, chains to support a ship's mast

Rudder: A flat, hinged piece on the stern of the boat. Used for steering

Sailmaker's Cabin: Place on the ship for storage and repair of sails

Saloon: A large cabin for common use. Often used for meals. On Star of India, it was an area for first-class passengers and officers

Skylarking: horseplay, being distracted, or passing the time with pranks

Slush fund: Money for bribing or money set aside for fun. For sailors, especially in the 18th century, it may refer to the fat or slush taken off the top when boiling salted meat. Sometimes the cook would save this and then sell it for extra money

Square meal: Large meal that meets all the food group requirements. In nautical terms, this may refer to the square trays or plates meals were on.

Starboard: Right side of a boat

Stern: Back of the boat

Tacking: Turning the bow of the boat through the wind, so the wind changes from one side of the ship to the other side

Take the wind out of his sails: To frustrate or undermine someone. This is from one boat getting in front of the wind of another ship, thus stealing the wind and making it so the ship slows down

Touch and go: Things are hard in a tricky situation. It refers to when a ship was in shallow water, scraping the bottom, but didn't ground itself

Yards: A cylindrical spar, tapering to each end, slung across a ship's mast for a sail to hang from

Paranormal Terms

Animal Spirits: Some have seen animals who have passed on, often beloved pets. Many owners report sensing their pets after the pet's death.

Cold Spots: Spots that feel 'cold' compared to the rest of the room or area. People sensitive to spirits usually experience these more intensely than others.

Crisis Spirits: A form of repetitive spirits formed after a crisis. They tend to be seen on the anniversary or around the crises' date. These experiences are often terrifying as the spirits themselves relive the situations that created them. Sometimes these can happen at the moment of a crisis, the moment of the person's passing. They may visit their loved ones in the moment of death or just before as a quick goodbye.

Demons: Demons are defined as fallen angels, though some debate this piece of theology. Demons are shapeshifters and manifest in many forms. Some manifestations are full-body apparitions. Others are black fog or mist. Some embodiments are ugly or beautiful. Often a foul odor like sulfur, sewage gas, or rot is reported around demons, though some say it's a spicy and not unpleasant smell. There is some debate about demons' purpose, whether they're causing havoc or breaking down humans for possession.

Divising (or Dowsing) Rods: Copper rods in the shape of an L used to communicate with ghosts. Generally, people use two at one time, held in the hands for the spirits to move in different directions to answer yes or no.

Ectoplasm: A fog often seen in photographs that may have ghostly connotations.

Electromagnetic Spectrum: It's thought ghosts can be seen using devices that look for different electromagnetic radiation types than our eyes can see. This is why you see ghost hunters using thermal cameras and electromagnetic detectors. It's thought that ghosts can disrupt the ambient electromagnetic field and trigger these devices.

EVP: Sounds recorded beyond the range of human hearing. Ghost hunters use these to collect evidence about hauntings. Ghost hunters will ask a series of questions while recording, hoping to capture the voice of a spirit upon review.

Funnel Ghosts: A photographic phenomenon where 'ghosts' are seen as funnels. Sometimes these are caused by photographer error and are merely particles of dust or bugs.

Intelligent, Sentient, or Interactive Spirits: These spirits are generally aware they're dead and will try to interact with the living, but may do it on their terms or through the filter of their historical experiences. For example, they may tell a woman to get out of an area that used to be men only. A child spirit may want to try to play with other children or may play pranks.

Orbs: A photographic phenomenon where "ghosts" are seen as translucent or opaque circles in the photo. Some feel orbs are merely bugs or particles of dust captured by the photographer. There is a lot of debate and analysis of these spheres in the ghost hunters community.

Poltergeist: A German word that means noisy spirit. Poltergeists are generally identified with spirit activity that is destructive and/or intense. Hauntings like these experience furniture moving, beds shaking and objects hurtling around, usually in front of witnesses. There's a lot of debate about whether or not poltergeists are entities or just destructive energy. Some claim poltergeists follow teenage girls or manifest as young girls begin puberty. This is a frightening haunting, but very rare.

Portals: These appear to be areas where ghosts move around to different realms, possibly "heaven" and "hell". Humans may experience this as cold spots or spots where strange creatures, such as Fae, or those identified as Fae may be.

Repetitive/Recurrent Spirits or Activity: The most common form of spirit activity. Ghosts are seen doing the same things they did in life, often pacing or walking through doorways. If the building changes, walls are built, or floors are raised or lowered, the ghosts won't respond. So you may hear stories of ghosts walking on floors on their knees (the floor was raised) or going into walls (there used to be a doorway there). Negative energy from an adverse event can also cause these, causing sensations of fear, anxiety, or sadness without a "cause". Festive events can do the same thing as can parties. Sometimes people will hear music, laughter, or music from a long-gone event.

Shadows: Shadows are usually seen as human shadow shapes without a cause. They're often wearing items like hats or clothing. Sometimes associated with feelings of dread or fear, many consider them non-human or never human. They have no facial features. Some report shadow animals, too, especially dogs and cats. On occasion, McBarnett has been thought to be a shadow spirit.

Bibliography

Arnold, Craig. 1988. Euterpe: Diaries, Letters and Logs of the *Star of India* as a British Emigrant Ship. San Diego: Maritime Museum Association of San Diego.

Burns, Phyllys B. 2003. Iron Lady at Sea. La Jolla.

Hendrickson, Robert. 1984. Salty Words. New York: Hearst Marine Books.

Macmullen, Jerry. 1961. Star of India: The Log of An Iron Ship. Howell-North.

Special thanks to the resources provided to us by the Maritime Museum of San Diego.

Scavenger Hunt

And now the hunt for answers is up to you! Want to conduct your own investigation aboard *Star of India*? Next time you visit the Maritime Museum during their hours of operation, capture the treasures below in photos, send us your shots, use these hashtags: #lostaboard #nbbp #StarOfIndia #MMSD, and tag us on Facebook @NBBPress! You may win a prize!

If you get stuck, ask one of the volunteers aboard for guidance. Get creative and have fun!

1. Is anyone there? Grab a shot peering through the Cook's Cabin's Window.
2. What's Cooking in the Galley?
3. From the deck, reach for the stars and point to the royal foreyard.
4. Sneak a peek into the first mate's cabin. Is McBarnett glaring back at you?
5. Steer her to safety! Snap a shot of yourself at the helm.
6. Prim and Proper - Imagine Yourself enjoying tea at the table in the saloon.
7. Is it cold in here? Find the foremast on the 'tween deck

and see if you can feel the presence of one of the spirits.

8. Long way up - snap a shot looking up to the top of the masts from the orlop.

9. Cooped up - how would you have entertained yourself on your journey to New Zealand from England?

10. What's that? Is that a meow? Can you find the cats aboard? *Star's* catheads were fashioned to honor the memory of Amy the cat, a longtime resident of the Maritime Museum during the early to mid-1980s.

11. Tied up - can you find the display of knots on *Star of India*?

12. Commandeer Your Vessel - set sail on the tiny-ship aboard.

13. This'll fit - find the portals used to bring timber aboard *Star of India.*

14. Artists Aboard - can you find the carvings in the ship that were made by fishermen who served during *Star of India's Alaska* Packer days?

15. Haul away! Turn the capstan!

16. Spirits of the fleet - are there any other places around the Maritime Museum where you feel like an unseen friend is with you?

About the Authors

Author S. Faxon, left, and Author Theresa Halvorsen, right, below decks on Star of India.

While being cooped up because of quarantine, Theresa and Sarah realized that they both wanted to write similar books about the histories and the ghost stories of some of their favorite places. Theresa wanted to write about Sacramento and Sarah wanted to write about the tall ship, *Star of India*. At the same time and due to the pandemic, they forged No Bad Books Press, a hybrid of both traditional publishing and independent services for authors. Their books, T*he Animal Court, Foreign & Domestic Affairs, Lost Aboard, River City Widows*, and *Tiny Dreadfuls* are their first-rounds diving deep into the publishing "practice."

Theresa Halvorsen, author of *Warehouse Dreams* and *River City Widows* lives in Temecula with her amazing husband, occasionally her college-age twins, and the pets they'd promised to care for. Find her at www.theresaHauthor.com

Sarah Faxon, author of *The Animal Court* and *Foreign & Domestic Affairs*, lives in San Diego with her life partner, too many statues of dragons, and her cat assistant, Bella Tuna Todd. For more from S. Faxon, visit her website at www.sfaxon.com

9 781735 726168